BECOMING ESSENTIAL

MAKING BRANDS UNIQUE

GUSTAVO FOLDVARI

AUTHOR OF "RETHINK THINKING"

This book is dedicated to:
My dearest wife Monica, our exceptional children, their beloved spouses, and our amazing grandchildren, to whom this legacy is all about.

WHAT YOU GET OUT OF THIS BOOK

Branding in the 21st century has grown more complex than ever before. Trust, which once served as a great ally of brands during the 20th century, now appears as a rare component in people's relationships with brands. Consumers and users demand more from their products and services, seeking constant advancement to the next level. They expect brands to actively improve their lives, going above and beyond the expected duty.

IN A MARKET SATURATED WITH CHOICES, becoming irresistible is crucial for a brand to stand out and thrive. The presence of choice might be appealing as a theory, but the reality is that people might find more choices to be debilitating. One of three things happen when people have too many decisions to make:
   1. Consumers end up making poor decisions;
   2. Consumers are more dissatisfied with their choices; or
   3. Consumers become paralyzed and don't choose at all.

. . .

When a brand is unique, it taps into deeper consumer desires and creates an emotional connection beyond satisfying basic needs or functions. This connection builds loyalty, as customers see the brand not just as a product or service but as an integral part of their identity or lifestyle. An essential brand does more than deliver quality—it offers a unique value proposition that resonates personally, setting it apart from competitors. In a crowded market, this appeal makes it easier for consumers to choose the brand repeatedly, reducing decision fatigue. It also drives word-of-mouth promotion as people naturally share compelling things across multi-channels, amplifying the brand's presence without requiring heavy marketing. In short, being unique helps a brand create lasting loyalty, boost its visibility, and maintain relevance, even as new options constantly emerge.

Becoming Essential demonstrates different ways for brands, products, and services to become essential and indispensable, even in today's harsh market environment. Essential brands must climb Mount Everest, reaching only Camp 4, the last stage the Sherpas refer to before reaching the mountain's peak.

People deepen their engagement with brands through the four stages to reaching Camp 4:

1. Share of Wallet: A purely transactional interaction that is fast and fleeting without further connection.

2. Share of Mind: A rational connection, dry by nature, but valuable because the brand makes it onto a list of preferences.
3. Share of Heart: An emotional engagement where the brand gains a higher status, becoming short-listed and influencing decisions that might bypass rational considerations.
4. Share of Life: At this stage, all other "shares" become integrated, embedding the brand into people's lives without distinction between the brand and the individual.

THIS BOOK GUIDES your brand toward becoming a partner to consumers and users. It aims to anchor your brand offering on the ground of fundamental human needs and wants—the unavoidable.

INITIAL NOTE

Initial Note

THE AMERICAN MARKETING ASSOCIATION (AMA) defines a brand as a "Name, term, sign, symbol, or design, or a combination of these, that identifies the goods and services of one seller or group of sellers and differentiates them from the competition." When marketers create a new name, logo, or symbol for a product, they develop a brand. In the last century, people defined brands by the "4 Ps": product, price, promotion, and place. In this century, we have expanded that definition to "8 Ps, " including permission, proximity, perception, and participation. Today, a brand must possess:

1. Driving beliefs: The brand's values represent what the brand means and its source of relevance to individuals, society, and the environment.

2. Identification: The brand's personality shows its behavior and source of affinity with all the causes supporting its driving beliefs.
3. Benefits: The brand's territory outlines its business and source of income. It is about something other than geography but what area of consumption or service it owns, like a cereal brand owning breakfast.
4. Attributes: The brand's heritage demonstrates what the brand is and what its source of authority is.
5. Performance: The brand's ability to meet needs reveals what it is and its source of satisfaction.

AT ITS CORE, the brand's essence—its uniqueness factor and added value—will drive people to engage with and partner with it over the long term.

INTRODUCTION

Not all brands grow at the same rate, and not all products or services reach their full potential in market penetration, usage frequency, or customer bonding. The brands that achieve this success share one key factor: they become essential to their customers. The common thread among them is their primary, unavoidable, and critical role in individuals' lives.

Becoming Essential reveals the ten ways to become indispensable and integrate into people's lives. Sebastian Jespersen from Forrester noted, "Companies that want to achieve a 'share of life' relationship with customers will need to do right by them—not just for a moment, not just for a campaign, but for life."

In this book, I share my journey of uncovering the deeper connections between needs, wants, and brand attachment. This search intensified as my work took me across the globe, allowing me to engage deeply with consumers and users to pursue the Holy Grail of essential brands. I led research and strategy for clients like Kraft, SC Johnson, Nivea, and Nestlé across five continents.

I am proud to present my discoveries, offering insights beyond professional analysis to explore the human need for a brand to help, nurture, promote, advance, and fulfill our desires. In this century, more than ever, brands serve not as crutches but as partners and motivators, enhancing and brightening our lives.

Welcome to the exploration!

HOW THIS BOOK IS STRUCTURED

Becoming essential top 10 ways:
1. Talk Survival
2. Achieve Ritualization
3. Stay Close
4. Deal with the Three Brains
5. Embrace Cultural Needs
6. Tell a Story of Values
7. Get the Right Code
8. Make it Easy
9. Facilitate Connectivity
10. Emphasize the Authentic

The flow of each way:
Foundation

1. The model or theory behind it.
2. Relevancy
   a. Why it's important
   b. Key motivations

c. Associated concepts

Case examples: Showing how each Becoming Essential (BE) way was applied to offerings beyond the expected categories in each chapter.

Learnings: A summary of action guidelines for the specific way.

Essential Recommendations: An owner's guide, helping to choose and successfully manage the ten "Becoming Essential" ways.

Essential Books: Each "Becoming Essential" way is rooted in proven theory and methodologies. The last part of this book provides further reading for those who would like to dive deeply into a given way.

1

Becoming Essential Way #1: Talk Survival

Foundation

The Model or Theory Behind It

"Talk Survival" focuses on foundational human needs, which remain omnipresent but unconscious unless necessity triggers them. We best visualize these needs through Maslow's pyramid. Maslow's Hierarchy of Needs, a psychological theory proposed by Abraham Maslow, organizes human needs into five levels that form a pyramid:

1. Physiological needs: We require food, water, and shelter for survival.
2. Safety needs: We seek security, stability, and protection from harm.
3. Love and belonging: We form emotional relationships, friendships, and social connections.
4. Esteem needs: We strive for respect, recognition, and self-worth.
5. Self-actualization: We pursue personal growth, fulfillment, and achieving our potential.

MASLOW BELIEVED that we must satisfy lower-level needs before focusing on higher-level ones. This progression highlights how foundational needs—such as food, shelter, and security—must first be met to create the stability required for deeper connections, personal achievements, and self-fulfillment. Without meeting these basic needs, we may struggle to concentrate on more complex emotional, social, or intellectual pursuits.

TARGETING basic needs (physiological and safety) at the pyramid's base aims to reach consumers who focus on basic needs for survival and protection. Marketers targeting these levels should emphasize practicality, reliability, and affordability. Targeting basic needs is often seen in industries such as:

- Food and Beverage: Companies market products by highlighting their ability to satisfy hunger,

provide nourishment, or offer convenience. Fast food chains, grocery stores, and healthy food brands address physiological needs directly.
- Healthcare and Personal Care: Products such as medicines, hygiene items, and health services address physiological and safety needs. Marketing campaigns stress benefits such as disease prevention, cleanliness, and general well-being.
- Financial Services and Insurance: Businesses that sell financial products like savings plans, life insurance, or home insurance appeal to the consumer's need for long-term security and peace of mind.
- Home Security and Automotive Safety: Companies offering security systems, alarms, or car safety features focus their advertising on protecting consumers, their families, and their property.

RELEVANCY

PHYSIOLOGICAL AND SAFETY needs are paramount to identifying survival's branding "sweet spots," which range from the core dimension of self to the immediate close family circle. Talk Survival zero in the primary sources of well-being: the nurturance of home and job/income security.

"Talk Survival" implies marketing strategies emphasizing survival themes, speaking directly to consumers' concerns about securing their basic physiological and safety needs. By addressing survival directly, brands can resonate more strongly with consumers' instincts to protect themselves and their families.

THE ESSENTIAL ELEMENTS contributing to well-being, particularly a secure home and stable employment, provide security and stability. A home meets physiological needs like shelter and food, while job security ensures a steady income to fulfill those needs consistently. Brands focusing on real estate services, home improvement, career development, or unemployment insurance engage directly with consumers' core safety concerns.

GOOD NEWS: Your brand can become essential regardless of your category, product, or service. Once you understand the basic tenets of survival and well-being, reaching the sweet spot within your business category is possible.

YOUR BRAND HAS the potential to become essential, regardless of the specific category, product, or service it represents. By mastering the foundational principles of survival and well-being, you can create a brand that goes beyond transactional interactions and connects on a fundamental, human level. These principles highlight universal core needs and desires, such as security, comfort, and the pursuit of happiness. When your brand aligns with these intrinsic motivators, you transform it from a mere choice among many into a trusted and valued presence in people's lives.

. . .

ACHIEVING this requires a nuanced understanding of what makes people feel cared for, safe, and supported. By embedding these elements into your brand's identity and messaging, you can reach the sweet spot within your category, where your offerings meet deeper psychological needs. This strategic alignment fosters a sense of reliability, making your brand a natural choice that customers turn to instinctively. In this way, your brand evolves from just another option into a vital, dependable part of consumers' routines, ingraining itself in their lifestyles and ultimately becoming essential.

AT THE *SURVIVAL* LEVEL, the following psychological motivations are crucial to understand and cater to:

- **Shielding:** The most critical umbrella motivation.

- Personal health
- Personal security
- Family health
- Family security
- Property security
- Job/income continuity

Related marketing concepts are:

- Safety
- Well-being
- Family
- Body shielding
- Real-life design or formulation.
- Useful tech
- Reliability

Case Examples
> Apple Watch and iPhone health and safety features
> Apple Watch: An essential post-launch strategic shift

Background

When Apple launched the Apple Watch in 2015, it marketed the device as a versatile smartwatch focused on notifications, fitness tracking, and communication. While it included some health-related features like basic heart rate monitoring and activity tracking, these weren't the main selling points at the time. Over the years, Apple shifted its strategy to make health monitoring the primary focus of the Apple Watch. This change started with the introduction of more advanced health tools.

One of the first significant upgrades was the ECG app in Series 4 (2018), which allowed users to take an electrocardiogram directly from their wrist. This feature turned the

Apple Watch into a more professional health device, capable of detecting atrial fibrillation, a potentially dangerous heart condition, and offering a more accurate way to monitor heart health. In the same series, Apple added Fall Detection, a feature aimed at a broader audience, especially older adults. It could automatically contact emergency services if the wearer experienced a severe fall, adding a life-saving layer to the device.

As HEALTH TRACKING became more central to the Apple Watch's identity, the Series 6 (2020) introduced Blood Oxygen Monitoring. This sensor allowed users to check the oxygen levels in their blood, which became especially relevant during the COVID-19 pandemic when respiratory health became even more critical. Later that year, watchOS 7 added sleep tracking, further enhancing the Watch's wellness capabilities, though it wasn't as advanced as the heart rate or ECG features at first.

In 2022, the Apple Watch Series 8 introduced even more health-focused advancements, such as temperature-sensing technology. This feature was particularly useful for women's health, offering more accurate tracking of ovulation cycles. It marked another important step in Apple's focus on health monitoring. Over time, the Apple Watch has evolved from a general smartwatch to a more specialized health tool, with each new feature strengthening its role as a critical device in personal well-being.

Performance

. . .

IN FISCAL Q2 2023, Apple reported $8.76 billion in revenue from its wearables, home, and accessories segment, which includes the Apple Watch. This growth is a significant increase from previous years and reflects the strong demand for Apple Watch as a core driver of this category. By comparison, in 2017, this segment generated $5.1 billion, showing the rapid growth coinciding with the shift to health-focused features like the ECG (2018) and fall detection.

Achievements

APPLE'S MARKETING increasingly emphasizes the importance of health and safety features to the watch. The ability to monitor heart health, detect falls, and connect with emergency services has resonated strongly with consumers. High-profile stories of the Apple Watch detecting heart irregularities or helping save lives in emergencies have amplified its reputation as a life-saving device, contributing to increased sales momentum.

APPLE CONSISTENTLY HOLDS a dominant position in the global wearables market. As of 2022, the Apple Watch made up around 30% of the worldwide smartwatch market, maintaining its status as the top-selling smartwatch. No other company matches Apple's share in this space, primarily attributed to its health and safety features. By 2023, the Apple Watch had sold over 100 million units since its launch, with health-related innovations playing a critical role in driving these sales numbers.

iPhone: An essential feature promoting "satellite safety"

Background

The Emergency SOS via Satellite feature, introduced with the iPhone 14 series, allows users to make emergency calls and send texts without cellular or Wi-Fi coverage. This feature is especially useful in remote or rural areas where traditional communication options are unavailable.

How it works: When users are out of reach of cellular or Wi-Fi networks and need help, their iPhone connects to low-Earth orbit satellites. The phone then helps users position the device correctly for the best signal, as satellite connections can be slower and require precise alignment. Once aimed correctly, the iPhone sends an emergency message with location details and information about the situation to relay centers, which then connect the user to emergency services. The system optimizes the message to send it efficiently, ensuring help arrives as quickly as possible, even with the low bandwidth of satellite communication. It compresses the data to send a quick but important message, including the user's location and medical ID details, making it easier for rescuers to find them faster. Users can also share their location through the Find My app, letting family or friends track them, even when they're off the grid.

The Emergency SOS via Satellite feature significantly impacts both safety and the market. For safety, it's a game-changer for people in remote areas, like hikers, travelers, or those living in places with few cell towers. It offers an extra layer of protection by making sure emergency services are accessible no matter where you are. This feature provides peace of mind for outdoor adventurers or anyone in remote locations, knowing help is within reach, even in life-threatening situations where regular networks won't work.

This feature sets the iPhone apart from competitors in terms of market impact. It offers a safety function that others don't, which is a big draw for customers, especially those into outdoor activities. It also enhances Apple's reputation as a brand focused on user safety. With features like Emergency SOS, Medical ID, and crash detection already in place, the addition of satellite communication strengthens Apple's position, appealing to consumers who prioritize safety. The release of this feature with the iPhone 14 in September 2022 has generated a lot of buzz and helped drive sales as demand for safety features continues to rise.

Performance

According to a survey, a significant percentage of consumers (around 55% to 70%) expressed interest in purchasing a smartphone with emergency communication features, highlighting how safety innovations can drive buying decisions. Apple reported strong demand for the iPhone 14 series, with overall sales exceeding expectations. In the fourth quarter of 2022, Apple sold over 100 million iPhones, partially attributing this success to the new safety features, including satellite communication. Analysts noted that the iPhone 14 series experienced a 12% increase in sales during its launch compared to the previous model, with safety features likely contributing to this uptick.

SINCE ITS LAUNCH on October 13, 2023, the iPhone 15 has had impressive sales figures, significantly outperforming the iPhone 14. Reports indicate that in the first four weeks after its release, the standard iPhone 15 sold more than double the units sold by the iPhone 14 in the same timeframe. Overall, total sales of the iPhone 15 series were 41.9% higher than those of the iPhone 14 series during the initial weeks.

BECOMING ESSENTIAL FACTOR: Focus on Safety

AS SATELLITE COMMUNICATION TECHNOLOGY EVOLVES, Apple plans to expand these features in future models, increasing interest and driving sales. This focus on emergency communication aligns with broader consumer electronics trends, where companies increasingly prioritize safety and security. While specific sales figures directly linked to the satellite communication feature might not be available, it has boosted the appeal of the latest iPhone series. This feature has helped Apple see increased sales and strong market performance by aligning with consumer interests in safety. Apple's innovative take on emergency communication has given it an edge over competitors in the smartphone market.

APPLE'S SAFETY features stand out not just for its advanced technology but also for its commitment to user well-being and emergency response. Apple ensures that personal health and safety data stays private. Unlike other platforms that might expose data, Apple securely stores and encrypts health app and emergency feature information.

LEARNINGS

HOW TO MAKE it work "Talk Survival" in your offering:

- Key Customer Driver: Shielding from aggressive external agents.
    - At the safety level, people seek solutions that reassure them of reliable performance in moments of need. Like the digital world, it operates on absolute values of zeros and ones, with no room for uncertainty, and a safe offering guarantees to meet expectations every single time.

- What to Identify: Physiological and safety "sweet spots."

- A sweet spot precisely reflects your offering and aligns with customers' expectations. Safety forms the foundation of all needs, rooted deeply in primal instincts that extend beyond psychology to the physiological and instinctive. Every offering, service, or product includes a safety component, visible or hidden. Identifying this safety element early on allows it to deliver meaningful rewards sooner.

- "Essential" Insert: Unavoidable self-defense or well-being component.
  - The word "insert" captures the essence: you don't need to completely redesign your offering, which is usually impractical outside of safety-specific products or services, like those offered by alarm companies. An insert means that once you identify the safety need in your business category, you choose a component to add that reflects this essential need. Amazon ensures peace of mind with easy returns, IKEA supports its customers with the "Love it or return it" program and Blue Apron reassures customers with a "Freshness guaranteed" promise.

- Key Customer Reward: Credible protection

- We must all acknowledge that trust in marketing has nearly disappeared today. Brands have overused customer confidence, leaving only a slim margin of credibility. Safety and protection mean little if they're empty promises or superficial additions to an offering. A solid, credible feature must stand out when addressing these fundamental needs. Don't just claim it—demonstrate it.

- Brand Becomes: A need
  - When we make any shopping list, some of the articles we can do without. Others are good to have. A few are must-haves. We need to get the shortlisted ones; there is no other way around. If your offering, in any category, product, or service, reaches this position, it means that the customer can't live without it. Welcome to Nirvana.

IN SUMMARY:

YOU WILL UPGRADE your offering from "necessary" to "a must."

2

Becoming Essential Way #2: Achieve Ritualization

Foundation

The Model or Theory Behind It

Ritualization goes beyond simple routines. While routines focus on practicality, rituals are more emotionally charged. Take a morning coffee, for instance—it can either be a quick caffeine fix or a meaningful pause for reflection and planning. This difference lies at the core of ritualization.

Through repeated behaviors, ritualization taps into primal instincts and survival mechanisms. What started as essential habits can become deeply ingrained actions that continue shaping how we function today. We see this in cherished traditions, from religious practices to everyday routines, like a morning ritual. Ritualization adds ease by removing the need to think about recurring tasks, creating a flow, and often building an expectation for positive change.

Ritualization is rooted in anthropology and psychology, suggesting that people create rituals to give structure and meaning to time. We develop a sense of control, consistency, and identity by anchoring parts of the day or week in repeated actions. This concept applies to everything from formal ceremonies to personal habits, providing emotional and mental benefits.

Rituals help mark transitions, signify preparation, or serve as grounding techniques in everyday life. That morning coffee or evening journaling ritual might seem minor, but it offers a calm, predictable start or end to the day, which can ease the mind and reduce anxiety. Rituals allow us to pause, bringing order to our lives and helping us reconnect with ourselves or a broader purpose. Recognizing these sequences helps the mind smoothly transition into focused, relaxed, or prepared states, depending on what the ritual intends.

Relevancy

Psychologically, rituals help manage anxiety by turning the unpredictable into something controlled. Athletes, for instance, often follow pre-game routines to get in the zone, reducing stress and boosting performance. Similarly, students or professionals might create work or study rituals that prime their focus, marking a shift from relaxation to concentration. These rituals essentially prime the brain, enhancing productivity by setting a mental boundary. In relationships, ritualization shows up in regular activities or symbolic gestures that build connection, like weekly date nights, family meals, or holiday traditions. These rituals create shared memories and a sense of closeness.

Rituals have a unique power to transform through stereotyped actions—gestures, words, and objects that symbolically support a person's goals or aspirations. People embed personal and social rituals in their routines, making them automatic anchors of emotional balance and a sense of security, especially during uncertain times. By creating intentional moments of meaning, rituals help people feel grounded, peaceful, and resilient.

Ritualization also applies to brand relationships, creating a three-tiered experience that reflects a user's commitment level:

1. Habitual: This is mainly transactional, providing positive feelings toward the brand.
2. Routine: A halfway stage with functional satisfaction. Many brands mistake this for the highest level of attachment.
3. Ritualization: The top tier, where the brand becomes irreplaceable by offering something unmatched by others.

IN MARKETING, ritualization is a powerful tool for deepening brand loyalty by transforming consumer interactions with products into meaningful, repeatable experiences. Brands aim to develop "brand rituals" that integrate their products seamlessly into consumers' everyday lives, encouraging a sense of consistency and attachment. These rituals go beyond mere product use; they become special moments that provide emotional or psychological satisfaction, whether it's a morning pastry, an evening skincare routine, or a particular drink to celebrate a small success.

Researchers in marketing and consumer psychology examine how brands can achieve this level of ritualization through emotional branding and experience marketing. Emotional branding creates a deep, personal connection between the consumer and the brand, building feelings of comfort, nostalgia, or identity around a product. This connection is especially effective when the brand becomes associated with positive, repetitive activities or moods, like feeling energized, relaxed, or accomplished. Experience marketing, on the other hand, focuses on crafting an immersive experience that links product use to specific settings or contexts, such as weekends, holidays, or dayparts.

By associating their products with these emotionally resonant moments, brands encourage customers to incorporate them into established routines, making them essential parts of daily life. In doing so, the brand becomes more than just a product or service —it becomes a trusted companion in moments that matter, reinforcing loyalty and ensuring that consumers repeatedly reach for the same product.

AT THE *RITUALIZATION* LEVEL, the following psychological motivations are crucial to understand and cater to:

- **Delegation:** The most critical umbrella motivation.

- Relief
- Comfort
- Pleasure
- Anticipation
- Simplification

RELATED MARKETING CONCEPTS ARE:

- Reconnection
- Repetition
- Effortless
- Trouble-free
- Supportive

CASE EXAMPLE
Spotify

BACKGROUND

IT'S A WELL-KNOWN music streaming service that offers playlists and podcasts. These have become staples in people's lives, often integrated into morning routines, commutes, or workouts.

SPOTIFY WAS FOUNDED by Daniel Ek, former CTO of Stardoll, and Martin Lorentzon, co-founder of Tradedoubler, to offer a legal, user-friendly alternative to the music piracy that was everywhere, thanks to platforms like Napster and LimeWire. They saw that the rise in illegal downloads came from an apparent demand for affordable, on-demand music, so they set out to create a streaming service that could turn that demand into a sustainable business. Self-funding the project, they spent two years building Spotify, which launched as an invite-only platform in October 2008 in Sweden, the UK, France, and a few other European countries. The service offered free (ad-supported) and premium (ad-free, subscription) options, a model that would become central to its approach. In 2011, Spotify entered the U.S. market after securing deals with major American record labels, a big step that helped it increase in a new region. That same year, Spotify partnered with Facebook, allowing users to share their music activity on social media. This move helped expand its reach and attract more users through Facebook's massive network.

PERFORMANCE

SPOTIFY HAS EXPERIENCED impressive growth in recent years, seeing significant increases in its user base, market presence, and financials. By Q2 2023, the platform had surpassed 551 million active users, up from 515 million in Q1, and its premium subscribers grew by about 17% year-over-year, reaching 220 million. Spotify leads the global music streaming market, available in 184 countries, and offers an extensive catalog of over 5 million podcasts and 350,000 audiobooks. The 2022 acquisition of Findaway has played a vital role in this expansion, strengthening Spotify's position over competitors like Apple Music, Amazon Music, and YouTube Music, which are still fighting for market share.

Several factors contribute to Spotify's role as a daily essential for millions of users. The platform's personalized discoverability is a big draw, with advanced algorithms creating custom playlists like "Discover Weekly," which keep users coming back for fresh, tailored music. Spotify also offers playlists designed for specific moods or activities, such as a "Workout Playlist," encouraging regular use in people's daily routines. Its seamless integration across multiple devices, including phones, desktops, and smart speakers, ensures that users can access their music anytime, anywhere, while offline listening for premium subscribers adds extra convenience.

Spotify fosters a strong emotional connection by allowing users to create playlists tied to personal memories, helping them manage emotions, whether it's for stress relief, motivation, or relaxation. The platform also adds a social layer through user-generated and influencer-curated playlists, enabling connections through shared music tastes. With its diverse library of music and podcasts, including exclusive content, Spotify has become a one-stop destination for entertainment and information, keeping users engaged throughout the day. Additionally, introducing dynamic AI features, like the 2023 AI DJ, offers an interactive listening experience. This feature mixes music based on user preferences, offering commentary and blending familiar favorites with discoveries, adding a fresh and engaging layer to the Spotify experience.

Becoming Essential Factor: Focus on Personalization

Spotify has become a part of users' daily lives by offering deep personalization, easy accessibility, and intense emotional and social connections. What started as a streaming service has become a daily ritual. With features like curated playlists, personalized recommendations, and "Discover Weekly," Spotify tailors the experience to match each user's unique tastes and lifestyle. This customization level keeps users returning, making them less likely to switch to other services.

Spotify seamlessly integrates into different parts of a user's day, making music listening a more personal and meaningful experience. Whether commuting, working, exercising, or relaxing, Spotify offers playlists and mood-based suggestions that make finding the perfect soundtrack for any activity easy. This flexibility keeps Spotify relevant, making it a stable and mood-boosting part of everyday life.

Spotify also encourages social interaction through features that let users share playlists, follow friends and influencers, and discover music together. This social aspect creates a sense of connection, making music discovery more interactive and personal. By combining social features with music curation, Spotify enhances the individual experience while building stronger user connections, giving it a unique role in the social and emotional aspects of its audience's everyday routines.

IN SHORT, Spotify has deeply integrated itself into users' lives, becoming more than just a music app—it's a constant companion that tunes into moods, activities, and routines in natural and essential ways. By crafting playlists that reflect personal tastes, curating daily recommendations, and syncing seamlessly across multiple devices, Spotify moves with its users throughout the day. This thoughtful integration makes Spotify feel less like an external app and more like an extension of the user's lifestyle, effortlessly adapting to moments like commuting, exercising, or relaxing. This deep level of integration has elevated Spotify from a passive listening tool to a platform that shapes, enriches, and accompanies users' everyday experiences.

LEARNINGS

HOW TO MAKE it work in your offering:

- Key Customer Driver: Delegation of personal tasks.
    - When a brand becomes a "sure shot," the sky is the limit. Since it's a beachhead and the

start of a long-term relationship with its users, it's no small task to take over. While staying alert to competitors' copycats, the brand now has room to increase its reach by developing adjacent or complementary businesses.

- What to Identify: Ways for repetition and routine usage.
    - Pairing new habits with existing routines can be helpful, making the new habit feel like a natural part of the day. A reward system, either physical or emotional, will surely resonate with customers, increasing the odds of repeated transactions.

- "Essential" Insert: Brand proactive action, increasing embedment over time.
    - Ritualization will not happen if the brand shows no interest in connecting with its users. A habit and a routine aren't ritualization. Achieving the highest level requires strategic thinking and consistency over time. Lululemon is more than sports clothes; it symbolizes a healthy lifestyle. Starbucks offered the "third place," achieving deep loyalty and ritualization.

- Key Customer Reward: Comfort in reassurance.
    - Ritualization brings comfort and reassurance by creating a sense of stability and predictability. When a brand becomes a part of daily or weekly activities, it offers something familiar and dependable that users can count on. These repeated interactions establish emotional connections, as the brand becomes a comforting presence in users' lives, making them feel understood and cared for. This consistency reduces decision fatigue, allowing users to relax and have a reliable experience where they know what to expect. This fosters peace of mind and enhances their overall well-being.

- Brand Becomes: A daily companion.
    - A ritualized brand becomes a daily companion by embedding itself into meaningful moments and rhythms in a user's day, offering familiarity and value beyond mere function. When a brand consistently aligns with a customer's needs—whether for comfort, inspiration, or efficiency—it gains a special place in their life. Over time, users turn to it almost instinctively, trusting it to bring a sense of continuity and ease that makes each day feel more connected and complete.

IN SUMMARY:

YOU WILL UPGRADE your offering from "frequency of usage" to "routine embedment."

3

Becoming Essential Way #3: Stay Close

Foundation

The Model or Theory Behind It

Imagine the Sun is a given brand, and the orbiting planets are the customers, each with a different profile, but all orbit around the star. Gravity pull, or gravitational force, is the force of attraction that pulls two objects toward each other. This force is responsible for keeping planets in orbit around the Sun.

A gravity pull in life emerges from a clear, consistent beacon, providing direction and purpose. This beacon isn't just about who or what someone is; it's about how it reflects something meaningful and aligns with how people want to live. When this pull is strong, it naturally draws individuals toward experiences, routines, or groups that feel intuitive and satisfying and effortlessly integrate into their daily lives.

This pull stabilizes, offering a sense of reliability in a world of distractions and uncertainties. It simplifies decision-making by narrowing the focus to what fits and feels right, helping people avoid overwhelm. Over time, this alignment creates a rhythm where these experiences or associations become part of the person's foundation, allowing them to stay centered and committed to what truly matters without constantly questioning their path.

Relevancy

We regularly deal with issues as we evolve into highly mobile and time-starved individuals. We rely on "close friends," trusted partners who share one common trait: they stay close to us, retaining attractiveness and provoking a "gravity pull." Two prominent and intertwined forces drive this closeness: accessibility and attraction. Accessibility refers to immediacy and pervasiveness, while attraction brings interest and liking, encouraging recurring contact. These forces create an indent in mental options, pulling consumers close repeatedly, much like gravity. The result is the consumer's long-term commitment to the brand.

ONE KEY COMPONENT of staying close to customers is reducing mental strain, transforming it into ease of choice. Customers don't waste time comparing multiple options when a brand is known for dependability; they go straight for the dependable brand that assures a good outcome. For example, many consumers choose Neosporin for first aid because of its reliable quality. Similarly, when it comes to home cleaning products, people often opt for Clorox, trusting its reputation for effectiveness and reliability. Consumers also frequently choose Apple products, not only because of their innovative features but because of the dependable quality and seamless ecosystem that makes choosing them an automatic decision.

IN THE SERVICE SECTOR, the same principles apply. For instance, Instacart provides convenience and reliability for customers seeking grocery delivery. The platform's fast and dependable service allows customers to skip the hassle of in-store shopping, making it a go-to choice. Similarly, Netflix has become the automatic choice for streaming services. With its vast library, personalized recommendations, and reliable streaming quality, customers know exactly what to expect, which makes it easier to choose Netflix over competing platforms. Amazon Prime offers a similar service-based experience, with its fast delivery, exclusive content, and reliable customer service, ensuring repeat usage.

PART OF EASING choices is an automatic preference, where dependability makes a brand the "automatic choice" for customers, even without heavy promotions. When customers trust a brand's reliability, they often default to it, reducing the impact of competitors' marketing efforts. For instance, despite the range of competing options in the smartphone market, Uber's consistent reliability and user-friendly interface often make it the default choice for many. Dependable service-based brands like Dropbox enjoy similar automatic preferences. Their users know they can expect consistent, uninterrupted service, reducing the decision-making process to simply accessing their platform.

Dependable brands benefit from social proof, as satisfied customers share positive experiences online. This credibility boosts marketing efforts, providing potential customers with evidence of the brand's trustworthiness. Brands like Amazon, known for fast shipping, further demonstrate how customer experiences shape long-term loyalty. Satisfied customers often recommend these services to friends and family, expanding the brand's reach and reinforcing their position as the first choice in their category.

At the *attraction* level, the following psychological motivations are crucial to understand and cater to:

- **Dependability:** The most critical umbrella motivation.

- Shelter
- Credibility
- Familiarity
- Warmth
- Dependability

Related marketing concepts are:

- Center of gravity.
- Automatic
- Reputation
- Relationship
- Attractive
- Risk-free

CASE EXAMPLE
Casper

BACKGROUND

CASPER WAS FOUNDED 2014 by Philip Krim, Neil Parikh, T. Luke Sherwin, Jeff Chapin, and Gabriel Flateman to transform the traditional mattress industry. The company wanted to simplify the mattress shopping experience by focusing on online sales and offering a single, high-quality mattress model that would be shipped directly to customers in a compact box. This "bed-in-a-box" model allowed Casper to bypass mattress showrooms and offer a lower price, attracting widespread attention.

The company's initial launch was highly successful, with over $1 million in sales in its first month. Casper leveraged digital marketing, social media, and word-of-mouth to grow its customer base. Its early success helped it secure venture capital funding, allowing it to expand its product line to include pillows, bed frames, and other sleep-related products. Casper's approach resonated with a new generation of online shoppers, and by 2016, it had become a well-recognized brand, moving from purely online to retail partnerships and physical stores.

A NEW GENERATION of online shoppers—primarily Millennials and Gen Z—fueled Casper's rise, as they preferred the convenience and transparency of online purchasing over traditional in-store experiences. They found traditional mattress shopping cumbersome, with high-pressure sales and overwhelming options. Casper disrupted this experience by offering a single flagship mattress at a transparent price, shipped conveniently in a box. The brand used humor and pop culture references to engage this demographic through clever social media marketing that resonated with their interests in wellness and self-care. Casper's direct-to-consumer model enabled rapid product development based on customer feedback, while transparent pricing and a 100-night risk-free trial reduced purchase anxieties.

PERFORMANCE

BY MEETING SHOPPERS' growing expectations for speed, simplicity, and emotional connection, Casper changed the mattress industry and became a symbol of modern, customer-focused commerce.

. . .

In 2020, Casper went public but quickly ran into challenges. The brand faced pressure as competition in the mattress-in-a-box market grew, and the overall sleep product industry became overcrowded. Casper was acquired in 2022 by Durational Capital Management, which brought the company back to a private ownership model. This shift reflects both the disruptive power of e-commerce in traditionally brick-and-mortar industries and the harsh realities of scaling up in a saturated market. Casper's success, despite these challenges, inspired a wave of similar companies, leading to a complete transformation in how people purchase mattresses and sleep products today.

To stay competitive in the crowded market, Casper took several vital steps. First, the brand shifted from a purely online, direct-to-consumer model to include physical retail spaces. By partnering with stores like Target and opening its showrooms, Casper allowed customers to experience the mattresses in person, as many customers still need to physically test the product before making such a necessary purchase. The ability to touch and try the mattresses helped build confidence and led more consumers to take the plunge.

Casper didn't stop there; it diversified its product line to stand out even further. Beyond its flagship mattresses, the company began offering sleep-related products, including pillows, bed frames, and bedding. This move allowed Casper to cater to different customer needs and expanded its reach. The brand introduced new mattress models tailored to various budgets and sleep preferences, enabling it to compete more effectively with other companies offering multiple options.

At the same time, Casper worked hard to improve the overall customer experience. It strengthened its customer service and return policies to ensure that buyers felt supported every step of the way. The brand kept its signature 100-night trial, giving customers peace of mind and encouraging hesitant buyers to try the product risk-free. Casper also focused on creating a seamless shopping experience, whether customers were purchasing online or in-store, making it easier to shop and return items across both platforms.

On the marketing front, Casper leaned into a strong, relatable brand image. The company used humor, wellness-driven messaging, and content that resonated with younger audiences to create a loyal customer base. By positioning itself as more than just a mattress company—offering comfort, a better night's sleep, and an approachable personality—Casper built a connection with its customers beyond the product itself.

Finally, with new leadership, Casper turned its attention to improving profitability. The company focused on reducing operating costs and enhancing its store operations. Part of this involved creating a "culture of frugality" to streamline expenses while enhancing store productivity. For instance, Casper implemented a commission-based model for store associates, which helped motivate staff to drive sales and improve the overall performance of the physical locations.

Through all these efforts, Casper has remained a key player in the mattress market, adapting to changes and continuing to grow despite the challenges. Its journey highlights the importance of staying flexible and finding new ways to connect with customers, all while balancing growth and profitability in a competitive landscape.

Becoming Essential Factor: Focus on Closeness

The relationship between marketing closeness and a direct-to-consumer (DTC) approach plays a crucial role in how brands engage with customers, especially in today's competitive marketplace. DTC brands like Casper use this model to create stronger, more personal customer relationships. Cutting out intermediaries allows them to design tailored marketing strategies that speak directly to their target audience's needs, desires, and values.

A significant benefit of this closeness is the ability of DTC brands to gather and analyze customer data directly. Without intermediaries, brands can track real-time feedback, preferences, and behaviors. This wealth of data allows them to customize their marketing efforts, refine product offerings, and adjust messaging to match the evolving needs of their consumers. This level of personalization makes customers feel heard and valued, creating a feedback loop where they know their opinions influence the brand's decisions. As a result, customers develop a stronger sense of loyalty because they see the brand as responsive and committed to their satisfaction.

THE DTC MODEL also makes it easier for brands to tell their story and build a more authentic connection with customers. Through channels like social media, blogs, and email marketing, brands can openly share their company's values, missions, and human side. This transparency fosters emotional connections as consumers increasingly look to align themselves with brands that reflect their beliefs. Casper's marketing focuses on wellness and sleep education, positioning the brand as a mattress seller and a trusted partner in a consumer's health journey. This approach resonates deeply with customers, creating more than just a transactional relationship that feels personal and supportive.

CASPER HAS the unique advantage of controlling the entire customer journey—from initial marketing and purchasing to post-sales service. This control allows them to create a seamless, unified customer experience. They can deliver personalized messaging, quickly respond to customer inquiries, and make real-time product adjustments based on direct feedback. This level of attention helps brands build stronger relationships with customers, making them feel more connected and valued. It also increases customer satisfaction because brands can adapt quickly to their needs and concerns, which traditional retailers with complex supply chains and third-party interactions often struggle with.

CASPER'S APPROACH fosters marketing closeness by enabling brands to interact directly with consumers, deliver personalized experiences, and engage in authentic storytelling. These elements are crucial for building long-term loyalty and trust. In a world where consumers are constantly bombarded with choices, brands that can connect personally—by understanding customer needs, offering value, and providing seamless experiences—are more likely to stand out and thrive in today's crowded market.

LEARNINGS

HOW TO MAKE it work in your offering:

- Key Customer Driver: Dependability and credibility.
    - Once trust develops, the brain accepts one brand as its go-to option. This preference happens through the brain's reward system, which responds positively whenever a brand meets expectations. Consistent, satisfying interactions build brand familiarity and loyalty, reducing the brain's impulse to explore alternatives. Trust also decreases cognitive effort—relying on a familiar brand

becomes a shortcut, saving the brain from repeatedly evaluating options. Over time, the brand becomes the default choice, embedding it in the brain's reward patterns and reinforcing attachment.

- What to Identify: Points of accessibility and attraction.
    - The key to "Stay Close" is offering differentiating features and paying attention to the drivers of trust. Samsung, with all its strengths in quality and innovation, emphasizes reliability. Samsung provides extensive customer support, with service centers and warranties that cover repairs and troubleshooting. This after-sales service gives consumers confidence that the company stands behind its products and will assist them if issues arise. In short, Samsung will continue staying close to you.

- "Essential" Insert: Openness, transparency, and familiarity.
    - Nobody is perfect, not even big brands. When issues happen, and sooner or later, they will, they are open to explaining what happened and how it will get fixed. Transparent brands encourage and showcase customer reviews,

both positive and negative, as well as ratings and testimonials. This openness is common on platforms like Amazon, where vetted buyers can leave detailed feedback, helping potential buyers make informed decisions.

- Key Customer Reward: A trusted partner.
  - Unique and essential brands are more than shortcuts because they categorize customers as lazy decision-makers. On the contrary, a brand shortcut is earned through the whole user experience rather than by a few factors. A brand that becomes a partner achieves a place in our daily lives and, by doing so, learns and adapts to users' evolving requirements.

- Brand Becomes: A sure thing.
  - Education or self-improvement are seen as "sure things" because the trust invested always pays off in personal well-being and opportunities. A "sure thing" in marketing relates to the "last mile" concept, representing how a brand curates its experience across all customer touchpoints. The "last mile" is where a brand's reliability is most visible and measurable, making it a critical opportunity to reinforce its promise as a "sure thing" to customers.

. . .

IN SUMMARY:

YOU WILL UPGRADE your offering from "omni-access" to "inviting."

4

Becoming Essential Way #4: Deal with the Three Brains

FOUNDATION

THE MODEL or Theory Behind It

WHENEVER WE STRUGGLE between saving money or buying a new shirt, we deal with our "three brains." In this case, our decision-making process requires an agreement between the three brains.

In the 1960s, neuroscientist Paul D. MacLean introduced the idea of the triune brain, suggesting that the human brain developed in three major stages. These stages resulted in three distinct but interconnected layers, each with its functions. According to this theory, each layer represents a step in the brain's evolution, with each new layer building on the functions of the previous ones and adding new capabilities. This view of the brain as a layered structure reflects its evolutionary past.

You've probably heard about the innermost layer, known as the "reptilian" or primal brain, thought to be the oldest part of the brain, responsible for essential survival functions like regulating the heartbeat and breathing. It also drives our instinctual behaviors, including aggression and dominance, which are critical for survival. Surrounding the primal brain is the "limbic system," often called the emotional or mammalian brain. This middle layer developed in early mammals and plays a considerable role in emotions, memories, and social behaviors. It allows us to form connections, respond to threats and rewards, and experience various emotions that guide our social interactions.

The outermost layer, known as the "neocortex," is unique to mammals and primarily developed in humans. This layer handles higher-level functions like reasoning, planning, and complex thought, allowing us to solve problems, create, and think abstractly. It's also the seat of self-awareness, giving humans the unique ability to reflect on our experiences and consider future possibilities.

These three layers create a hierarchical model showing how ancient survival mechanisms coexist with more advanced emotional and cognitive abilities. This blend allows us to respond to our environment flexibly, drawing on a range of instincts, emotions, and higher reasoning. Although MacLean's triune brain theory has been influential, many modern neuroscientists see it as somewhat simplistic because brain functions are deeply interconnected rather than confined to separate layers.

For this book, however, this simplified model provides a helpful framework for understanding how to tap into different parts of the brain to make a brand genuinely essential. A brand can resonate more fully with the diverse, layered human mind by engaging each layer—from primal instincts and emotional connection to higher reasoning.

Relevancy

The ideal way to build a powerful brand is to create a rich, multi-layered proposition that combines various compelling elements under a single, cohesive message. By offering something that appeals on multiple levels, the brand invites all three parts of the triune brain to engage, creating a sense of ease that encourages people to try the product.

To reach the primal brain, which drives our need for safety and stability, the brand starts with the basics: delivering high-quality, dependable products that consistently meet everyday needs. The brand instills a sense of security by offering reliability and safety, making customers feel they can rely on it repeatedly. This dependability builds natural loyalty as customers trust the brand for what they need most.

Then, the brand goes further by connecting with the emotional brain, the part that craves connection, meaning, and identity. The brand taps into consumers' more profound aspirations by crafting an appealing aesthetic, standing by specific values, and offering experiences that foster community. It might promote ideas of adventure, wellness, or a sense of belonging, allowing customers to align their identities with the brand. This connection makes the brand helpful and emotionally significant; it becomes a means of expressing who they are and what they care about.

FINALLY, the brand speaks to the rational brain by integrating values like sustainability, innovation, or ethical production into its practices. This clear, evidence-backed commitment to higher principles shows that the brand isn't just focused on profits and aligns with consumers' thoughtful, future-minded choices. When people see a brand dedicated to responsible, ethical practices, they feel reassured that it aligns with their intellectual and ethical standards.

With this multi-layered strategy, the brand becomes more than just a functional option; it becomes a trusted part of consumers' lives, seamlessly fitting into daily routines and personal values. The brand transforms into something essential by consistently delivering reliability, building emotional bonds, and standing for meaningful values. It moves beyond simple "brand loyalty" and becomes embedded with a "share of life," an integral part of the customer's world.

AT THE SATISFACTION LEVEL, the following psychological motivations are crucial to understand and cater to:

- **Harmony:** The most critical umbrella motivation.

- Trust
- Balance
- Strengthening
- Fulfillment
- Confidence

Related marketing concepts are:

- Suspended judgment
- Opportunity
- Serenity
- Educated decision
- Savvy-ness
- Conscious
- Well-rounded

Case Example
Yasso Frozen Greek Yogurt

Background

Amanda Klane and Drew Harrington, the founders of Yasso, were childhood friends with a shared passion for food and healthy living. Growing up together in Massachusetts, they always loved the idea of creating something that combined their interests. But the idea for Yasso didn't come until 2009 when they attended a week-long ice cream camp, a hands-on training in ice cream science and production.

IMMERSED in a world of frozen treats, Amanda and Drew realized that the frozen dessert aisle was entirely of indulgent options but severely needed more nutritious, great-tasting alternatives. They saw a clear opportunity: why not create a frozen dessert that was as satisfying as traditional ice cream but healthier?

WITH GREEK YOGURT booming in popularity at the time, thanks to its high protein content and creamy texture, they saw its potential as the perfect base for their product. Greek yogurt had the thick, creamy quality of ice cream, and it was packed with protein and probiotics, making it both delicious and nutritious. So, Amanda and Drew decided to take a chance on this vision, merging the health benefits of Greek yogurt with the fun and enjoyment of frozen treats.

THE JOURNEY from idea to launch wasn't easy. Amanda and Drew had to learn the ins and outs of yogurt production and the frozen foods industry, navigating everything from product development to food safety regulations. They spent countless hours in test kitchens, experimenting with different recipes and flavors to get just the right balance between creaminess, sweetness, and health benefits. They wanted to create a product that didn't compromise on taste but offered a healthier ice cream alternative. They perfected recipes, locked in delicious flavors, and refined the texture to get the satisfying "mouth feel" of a traditional ice cream treat.

I𝙽 2011, after two years of research, product development, and brand building, Amanda and Drew launched Yasso as the first frozen Greek yogurt brand on the market. The response was overwhelmingly positive, as consumers looking for a guilt-free, creamy dessert quickly embraced Yasso's offerings. The brand's name, "Yasso," was inspired by the Greek greeting "Yasu," meaning "hello" or "to your health," reflecting both the Greek yogurt base and the health-focused mission behind the brand.

Y𝙰𝚂𝚂𝙾'𝚂 innovative approach quickly caught on. The brand's popularity skyrocketed, with new fans raving about the flavors and texture that made it feel just as indulgent as ice cream. In less than five years, Yasso became one of the fastest-growing frozen novelty brands, generating over $50 million in revenue by 2016. Amanda and Drew didn't just stop at creating a successful product—they wanted Yasso to have a positive impact beyond the grocery store. To give back to the community and inspire healthy living, they launched the Game On! Foundation. This foundation supports health and wellness initiatives for people of all ages, embodying the Yasso philosophy that everyone deserves a healthy, active lifestyle. Through Game On!, Yasso sponsors community events, promotes fitness and nutrition programs, and continues to connect with fans on a more personal level, making the brand a recognized leader in taste and positive impact.

. . .

Performance

Yasso's recent surge in sales is no accident—it results from a careful strategy that balances innovation with consumer insight. In 2022, the brand achieved a staggering 124% growth rate, reflecting growing consumer demand for healthier indulgences and Yasso's ability to lead in that space. Landing on Inc.'s list of the 5,000 fastest-growing companies signaled to investors, retailers, and consumers alike that Yasso wasn't just a trend but a brand with serious staying power.

By 2023, Yasso was on track to break the $300 million mark in retail sales, representing a 60% increase from the prior year. This level of growth in such a short period speaks to how well the brand resonates with today's health-conscious, convenience-driven consumer. Yasso has successfully positioned itself as a go-to option for consumers who want a guilt-free treat without sacrificing taste. The numbers reveal that Yasso has tapped into a critical market segment: people who prioritize health and wellness but still crave indulgent experiences.

CEO Craig Shiesley's projection of Yasso's potential to reach a half-billion-dollar valuation in a few years isn't just optimism. It reflects the brand's growth trajectory and the broader trends in the food industry, where consumer interest in high-protein, lower-calorie treats continues to grow. The brand's consistent double-digit growth points to a business model that's both scalable and adaptable.

. . .

SEVERAL STRATEGIC MOVES support these impressive numbers. Yasso's commitment to product innovation has expanded its audience by introducing items like Chocolate-Dipped Bars, Sandwiches, Poppables, and Mochi. Each product caters to different consumer tastes and eating occasions, helping Yasso stand out in the competitive frozen novelty aisle. The variety also reinforces the brand as a lifestyle choice, not just a one-off treat, encouraging repeat purchases.

IN ADDITION, Yasso's recent packaging redesign has contributed directly to its sales success. The bold branding and larger logo help Yasso stand out on crowded freezer shelves, while clear calorie information appeals to health-conscious shoppers looking for transparency. The redesign alone lifted sales by 44% in the following six months, showing that intelligent, consumer-centric packaging can be as influential as product quality.

YASSO'S ACQUISITION by Unilever in August 2023 was another calculated step forward. For Unilever, Yasso represents a valuable addition to its premium, healthier snack portfolio, aligning perfectly with the shift in consumer preferences. This acquisition brings Yasso into Unilever's vast distribution network, making it easier for the brand to expand nationally and internationally. With Unilever's backing, Yasso gains more resources and reach, strengthening its position to become a household name.

. . .

BECOMING ESSENTIAL FACTOR: Permissible Indulgence

YASSO'S CEO, Craig Shiesley, explains that their strategic vision is to make Yasso the leading "better-for-you" frozen snack brand, aiming to grow at a pace three times faster than the industry. Yasso's growth strategy took shape as they capitalized on a unique consumer trend: the pandemic sparked a craving for comfort foods, but many people also wanted healthier, low-calorie choices. This mix of indulgence and health—what Shiesley calls "permissible indulgence"—continues to guide today's snacking habits and has become central to Yasso's appeal.

ONE KEY to Yasso's success is its ability to satisfy the brain's three layers of decision-making: primal instincts, emotions, and logic. Yasso's Greek yogurt bars deliver ice cream's creamy, indulgent experience but with fewer calories, less fat, and more protein, appealing directly to our primal need for comfort and enjoyment. They are a "safe" treat—a snack that tastes good without the guilt.

EMOTIONALLY, Yasso resonates by positioning itself as a go-to snack for any time of day and fostering a sense of community around wellness and healthy living. The brand's identity and values are tied to these health-driven aspirations, letting people indulge while staying aligned with their fitness goals or lifestyle. It's a feel-good personal and social experience, as customers see Yasso as part of a healthy lifestyle that's easy to share and enjoy.

. . .

FROM A RATIONAL PERSPECTIVE, Yasso adds extra value using Greek yogurt, which provides protein and probiotics. This meets consumers' desire for snacks that offer functional benefits. The brand's shift into new formats and flavors appeals to practical minds. As more people snack at home, Yasso's variety and accessibility make it a smart choice for health-conscious shoppers.

BY ADDRESSING all three decision-making areas—primal satisfaction, emotional connection, and rational value—Yasso has positioned itself as a frozen snack that tastes great and aligns with people's values and habits. This layered approach strengthens Yasso's position in a competitive market and prepares it well to reach its growth goals.

LEARNINGS

HOW TO MAKE it work in your offering:

- Key Customer Driver: Harmony. A well-balanced decision.
    - When purchasing, we usually engage in an inner dialogue: "I want it now" versus "Do I need it?" A guilt-free solution offers harmony. A balanced proposition answers all doubts, paving the way for the customer's favorable decision.

- What to Identify: Multi-layered positive propositions.
    - Every featured brand benefit or advantage must contain more than a single proposition. By blending primal satisfaction, emotional connection, and rational justification in their product benefits, L.L. Bean creates a layered experience that resonates with all parts of the brain. Each item isn't just functional; it's a piece of a larger story about nature, durability, and timeless quality. This multi-layered approach makes their products feel essential.

- "Essential" Insert: A holistic approach (not many scattered benefits).
    - Brands that take a holistic approach embed a consistent core philosophy or mission into every facet of the customer experience rather than focusing on a variety of isolated features or benefits. Holistic brands deliver a unified experience. Each interaction reinforces a cohesive message or lifestyle, from product design to customer service, advertising, and social responsibility. Examples are IKEA, Trader Joe's, and Method.

- Key Customer Reward: Satisfaction. Peace of mind.

- When we cater to the triune brain, we achieve peace of mind, giving ourselves the green light to enjoy our purchase fully. This approach creates a warm feeling toward the brand, allowing us to settle into a serene mental agreement with our choice.

- Brand Becomes: A three-layered win.
  - Brands that deal with the three brains center their entire identity and product experience around one core philosophy, aligning every feature, benefit, and interaction with a central, authentic purpose. The concept of a holistic brand approach wins every time because it builds a deeper, more lasting connection with customers by appealing to their whole selves, not just isolated desires or needs.

IN SUMMARY:

YOU WILL UPGRADE your offering from "all-inclusive" to "a self-contained whole."

5

Becoming Essential Way #5: Embrace Cultural Needs

Foundation

The Model or Theory Behind It

DNA SHAPES who we are at a chemical level, and culture acts as a second DNA, influencing our social behavior. This cultural DNA builds a framework of expectations and responsibilities beyond individuals, blending with biological DNA to shape consumer needs.

Cultural DNA models examine the core traits that make each culture unique, serving as blueprints for a group's identity, values, and behaviors. Like biological DNA, cultural DNA includes essential elements that shape how a group sees the world, interacts with it, and envisions its future. This "genetic code" comprises layers like history, beliefs, language, rituals, and symbols, defining a society, community, or organization's unique features. Each part is vital in holding the group together and guiding responses to challenges, opportunities, and changes over time.

Values and beliefs are also core to cultural DNA. Values act as a group's ethical guide, setting standards for what's honorable, desirable, or acceptable, while beliefs shape how members interpret the world around them. Together, they form the foundation of a culture's ideology, affecting everything from individual choices to collective goals. In diverse contexts, understanding cultural DNA fosters mutual respect, enhances communication, and encourages effective collaboration among different groups.

Cross-cultural interactions and exposure to different perspectives also drive cultural evolution, enriching a culture's values, practices, and adaptability. When people interact across cultural lines, they gain new insights into ways of thinking, problem-solving, and organizing social life. This exposure can inspire rethinking one's beliefs, sparking innovative solutions, expanded values, and a greater openness to change.

Relevancy

Cultural DNA evolves as people and groups navigate the gap between ideals and reality. Understanding this tension is essential to genuinely engaging with or influencing culture. It reveals the motivations behind a group's identity and the personal challenges of aligning individual experience with collective ideals. Cultural DNA becomes a roadmap to defining a group and reflects ongoing adaptation and personal balance when we understand this.

. . .

EXPOSURE to different cultural perspectives challenges stereotypes and biases. When people experience the nuances of other cultures, they often see past surface-level differences and gain a clearer sense of others' motivations and struggles. This exposure helps build a more inclusive culture, as people recognize that diverse experiences and viewpoints are crucial to a well-rounded society.

UNFORTUNATELY, bullying has also evolved with society, technology, and growing cultural awareness. It used to be limited to physical aggression, verbal abuse, or social exclusion in close-knit spaces like schools or workplaces. But as society became more connected and technology advanced, bullying shifted into complex, far-reaching forms—primarily online. This shift has transformed bullying from a local, often overlooked issue to a broad social problem demanding action in real and virtual spaces.

MOST PEOPLE SEEK inclusivity because it meets deep social and psychological needs for belonging, acceptance, and recognition. We're social beings, and feeling included connects us to others, giving us a sense of validation and boosting mental and emotional well-being.

When people feel valued, they're more likely to feel confident, happy, and motivated, strengthening their bond with the group. Inclusivity also fosters a space where people can express themselves openly, share ideas, and participate without fear of judgment. This respect is critical in diverse settings where people from different backgrounds come together. Inclusivity ensures people won't be sidelined for their differences, helping reduce anxiety and build psychological safety.

AT THE INCLUSIVITY LEVEL, the following psychological motivations are crucial to understand and cater to:

- **Affinity:** The most critical umbrella motivation.

- Sensible solution
- Improvement
- Belonging
- Respect
- Perfect fit
- Smart
- Self-esteem

RELATED MARKETING CONCEPTS ARE:

- In-sync
- Integration
- Community
- Safe choice
- Upgrade
- A better way

Case Example
Dove

Background

In the early 2000s, Dove noticed that the beauty standards in ads didn't reflect how most women saw themselves. Traditional beauty ads showcased unrealistic, heavily edited images of young, thin, flawless models, creating pressure and feelings of inadequacy. Dove saw an opportunity to change this and position itself as a brand that promoted authenticity and self-acceptance. This change led to the launch of their iconic "Real Beauty" campaign.

The shift started with research into how women viewed beauty and how it affected their self-esteem. Dove found that only a few women felt beautiful by media standards, and many were frustrated with the narrow, idealized portrayals of beauty. Seeing a need for a more inclusive definition of beauty, Dove changed its message to focus on diversity, uniqueness, and self-confidence.

In 2004, Dove launched the "Real Beauty" campaign, featuring real women, not models, with different ages, body types, and skin tones. By showcasing women who didn't fit traditional beauty standards, Dove sent a clear message: Beauty isn't about fitting into one mold but embracing individuality. The campaign encouraged women to appreciate their beauty and realize their worth beyond looks.

Dove also backed up this shift by creating a brand identity focused on more than just selling products. It invested in programs to boost self-esteem and fight negative body image, working with experts to develop resources for young women. The brand reached millions through projects like the Dove Self-Esteem Project, showing that "Real Beauty" wasn't just a slogan but about making a real difference.

Dove also adapted its media strategy by using digital platforms and social media. These channels allowed women to share stories, join conversations, and celebrate each other, creating a community connected by the message of self-acceptance. The campaign resonated worldwide, turning Dove from a beauty brand into a cultural voice advocating for a healthier self-image.

By abandoning traditional beauty ideals and promoting inclusivity and self-worth, Dove changed how brands connect with consumers. This strategy wasn't just a marketing shift; it aligned Dove's purpose with what its audience valued, building loyalty and influencing the beauty industry. The "Real Beauty" campaign became a cultural movement, setting a new standard for authenticity and social responsibility in advertising and inspiring other brands to follow suit.

Performance

Dove's *"Real Beauty"* campaign revolutionized the brand's trajectory, driving substantial sales and consumer preference growth while reshaping the beauty industry. Before the campaign's launch in 2004, Dove's performance was steady, with moderate revenue increases. However, the campaign catalyzed an extraordinary transformation. Within a decade, Dove's sales soared from $2.5 billion to over $4 billion, reflecting its ability to connect deeply with consumers. This surge in demand spanned critical product lines, mainly body wash and beauty bars, as the brand's message of inclusivity and empowerment resonated worldwide.

. . .

BEYOND FINANCIAL GAINS, the campaign redefined Dove's market position, elevating it from a standard beauty brand to a cultural touchstone with a mission. Dove challenged conventional norms by celebrating diverse beauty and rejecting the unattainable standards that had long dominated the industry. Surveys, focus groups, sales, and consumer feedback highlighted this shift, showing that customers now viewed Dove as a brand with purpose and authenticity.

THE CAMPAIGN FOSTERED a profound emotional connection with its audience, turning casual buyers into loyal advocates. By aligning its products and messaging with real-life experiences and values, Dove transformed itself into a brand that sold beauty products and inspired confidence and self-acceptance. This approach enhanced customer loyalty and attracted new audiences, further solidifying Dove's position as an industry leader committed to social impact and meaningful change.

BECOMING ESSENTIAL FACTOR: Cultural Resonance

CONSUMER PREFERENCE DATA revealed a powerful connection between Dove's messaging and audience. Engagement surged as the brand's social media presence expanded, fueled by enthusiastic interaction and positive feedback on its campaigns. The "Real Beauty" campaign ignited widespread online conversations, inspiring consumers to share their own stories of self-acceptance and body positivity. This dialogue amplified Dove's impact, creating a ripple effect of empowerment and inclusion.

Research on brand sentiment highlighted lasting positive associations, with consumers expressing stronger loyalty to Dove. The brand's consistent focus on authenticity and social initiatives starkly contrasted with competitors' traditional beauty campaigns, making Dove a beacon of purpose-driven marketing. The campaign's influence extended beyond Dove itself, inspiring other Unilever brands and companies to embrace socially conscious strategies, further positioning Dove as a pioneer in meaningful branding.

The long-term success of the "Real Beauty" campaign remains evident. Dove continues championing self-esteem and body positivity while holding a solid market position. By aligning its financial goals with its mission to promote confidence and inclusivity, Dove secured its place as a trusted and beloved brand for millions. The campaign not only drove substantial financial growth but also redefined the standards for beauty marketing, establishing Dove as a leader in purpose-led branding.

Learnings

How to make it work in your offering:

- Key Customer Driver: Affinity. A cultural voice.
  - Like an oasis in the desert, it is rare to find a brand that offers more than its category's benefits or even its particular points of formulation differentiation. A brand with a voice, a cultural impact, and an agent of positive change will undoubtedly become a loyalty magnet.

- What to Identify: Ways to reflect cultural needs.
  - Brands can tap into cultural needs by staying attuned to current events and cultural shifts, tailoring their offering and communications to resonate with audiences, and becoming a part of the cultural zeitgeist. TikTok (turning ordinary users into trendsetters), Heineken (the beer of connection and inclusivity), and TOMS ("One for One" model, aligning with values of social responsibility) are cultural icons for their respective audiences.

- "Essential" Insert: Integrating individual and cultural needs.
  - Mimicking the culture will not work. Addressing cultural needs requires a solid foundation rooted in actual values. A brand like Dove invested time in understanding the nuances of what beauty today should mean, avoiding superficial gestures.

. . .

- Key Customer Reward: Satisfaction. A better way.
    - Customers of these brands feel seen, valued, and inspired. They gain a sense of belonging, knowing their values align with the brand's actions. They enjoy products and experiences that reflect their identity, celebrate their culture, and support the causes close to their vest.

- Brand Becomes: Perfect fit
    - The essential tenets for a brand to become a perfect fit are a deep understanding of its audience, aligning its values with theirs, and consistently delivering authentic experiences that resonate with its identity and aspirations.

IN SUMMARY:

YOU WILL UPGRADE your offering from "customer needs" to an "empowering advocacy."

6

Becoming Essential Way #6: Tell a Story of Values

FOUNDATION

THE MODEL or Theory Behind It

SINCE INDIVIDUAL AND cultural needs are actual customer needs, values should serve as the third leg of the stool. With them, some types of propositions risk becoming unstable. From ancient times, people have relied on storytelling to pass down morals, ethics, and lessons in ways that resonate across generations. Fables and anecdotes distill complex ideas into memorable tales, transforming abstract values into something tangible and universally relevant. This storytelling tradition endures because it naturally illustrates consequences, shapes behavior, and reinforces shared beliefs without appearing preachy.

Storytelling is humanity's oldest tool, deeply embedded in how our brains process information. It engages us on multiple levels. Confucius captured this dynamic perfectly: "Tell me and I forget, show me and I remember, involve me and I understand." Annette Simmons expands on this in The Story Factor, identifying six types of storytelling, including stories about values. The others focus on identity, purpose, vision, teaching, and shared understanding. Stories centered on values create emotional connections, leaving lasting impressions.

Neuroscience backs this up. Stories activate multiple areas of the brain, making ideas both memorable and relatable. When listeners place themselves within a narrative, they naturally develop empathy and anchor shared values more deeply. Value-based stories resonate culturally, reflecting shared aspirations and strengthening collective identity. By weaving values into authentic narratives, storytellers—whether individuals or brands—connect with their audiences in meaningful and credible ways. Instead of instructing directly, stories show outcomes and consequences, encouraging reflection without feeling forced.

Our brains prefer information presented in story form because stories organize complexity into a coherent flow. Values expressed through storytelling stick with us because they make abstract principles concrete and more accessible to internalize. These narratives also influence behavior more effectively by bypassing typical resistance. They invite listeners to reflect on their beliefs and actions naturally and unforcedly. When a story embeds values, it gains the power to connect emotionally and inspire real-world alignment with these ideals.

Relevancy

The first step is to determine what customers truly value in your offer. Once you know that, the next step is to weave that value into a compelling and inspirational story that makes people care and want to get involved.

For stories to resonate without feeling like a hard sell, brands must focus on integrity and real human experiences. Customers can spot that a brand is genuine and appreciate it when a story is grounded in fundamental values instead of just another promotional pitch. When brands tell stories that reflect shared beliefs and challenges, they create a sense of community. Customers feel like they belong to something bigger, not like they're being marketed to.

In telling these stories, brands should showcase values through examples that anyone can relate to daily. Rather than focusing on products, it's the impact of these values on people that truly matters. Customers notice when a story touches on issues they care about—things like environmental responsibility, personal empowerment, or community support. It's not about shining a spotlight on the brand but about finding common ground, showing that the brand's values align with the values of its customers.

When brands make their storytelling relevant, they help customers see themselves as part of the story. In the narrative, customers who recognize their experiences or aspirations feel like the brand understands their journey. This relevancy builds trust and creates a genuine connection beyond transactions to lasting loyalty.

Take Ben & Jerry's, for example. They consistently use storytelling to highlight their commitment to social justice, environmental issues, and human rights. By aligning with causes like climate action and marriage equality, they earn the trust of customers who care about those issues, reinforcing the idea that Ben & Jerry's stands with them.

LEGO does something similar with its "Rebuild the World" campaign, highlighting creativity, imagination, and inclusivity. The brand emphasizes its core values of creativity and empowerment by telling stories of kids and adults building new worlds with LEGO.

Apple, too, excels with storytelling driven by values. For instance, its "Shot on iPhone" campaign celebrates personal expression and artistry, tying the brand to values of creativity and individuality while highlighting its commitment to environmental responsibility.

But not all brands get it right. In 2017, Pepsi faced significant backlash over an ad featuring Kendall Jenner, which tried to tap into social justice themes. Critics accused the brand of trivializing important issues and using them as a marketing tool. By turning social movements into a backdrop for selling soda, Pepsi's approach felt opportunistic and insincere. This unfortunate approach backfired because consumers could tell the story wasn't authentic, reminding us how important it is for brands to stay true to their values.

AT THE *VALUES* LEVEL, the following psychological motivations are crucial to understand and cater to:

- **Human-centered:** The most critical umbrella motivation.

- Integrity
- Believability
- Simple
- Concrete
- Uniqueness
- Caring

RELATED MARKETING CONCEPTS ARE:

- Shared values
- Shared humanity
- Pleasantly unexpected
- At a personal level
- Touching

CASE EXAMPLE
Patagonia

BACKGROUND

Patagonia started in 1973 when Yvon Chouinard, a passionate rock climber, turned his hobby into a small business selling climbing gear. Chouinard had been making his climbing equipment for years, focusing on quality craftsmanship that matched his love for the outdoors and need for reliable gear. As his reputation grew in the climbing world, so did the demand for his equipment. Early on, the business focused on creating gear tough enough to handle the challenges of the mountains.

By the late 1970s, Patagonia shifted its focus to outdoor clothing. Customers wanted gear that was not only functional but also stylish, and Chouinard's growing awareness of environmental damage shaped the company's direction. He wanted Patagonia to be about more than performance—it had to stand for sustainability, too. Patagonia became one of the first companies to use recycled materials in its clothing, setting the tone for its future.

In the 1980s, Patagonia introduced its iconic fleece jackets, which became a hit with outdoor enthusiasts. Around the same time, the company began speaking out about environmental issues, like reducing the impact of outdoor sports on nature. This commitment went beyond materials. Patagonia also focused on ethical business practices, such as paying fair wages to workers in its supply chain.

The 1990s and early 2000s saw Patagonia doubling down on its environmental efforts. The company launched the "1% for the Planet" initiative, pledging 1% of its sales to environmental nonprofits. It also started programs like "Worn Wear," which encouraged customers to buy used Patagonia products and repair their old ones to cut down on waste.

Over time, Patagonia became known as a brand and an activist force. It tackled issues like climate change and the protection of public lands. One bold move came in 2011 with the "Don't Buy This Jacket" campaign, where Patagonia asked customers to consider the environmental impact of their purchases. Instead of pushing for more sales, the campaign highlighted responsible consumerism, cementing Patagonia's reputation as a company that practices what it preaches.

Today, Patagonia remains a leader in sustainability and corporate responsibility. Its innovation in product design and environmental activism has earned it a loyal following of customers who see the brand as more than just a retailer —it's a force for positive change. Chouinard's vision of a business that balances success with a commitment to the planet continues to drive Patagonia forward.

Performance

Patagonia's sales success stems from a combination of innovative strategies and deep-rooted values. The brand thrives by telling compelling stories that emphasize its commitment to the environment, creating a solid emotional connection with its customers. Through initiatives like the Footprint Chronicles, Patagonia reveals its production process, offering customers a transparent look at how it makes its products.

This openness builds trust and reinforces the brand's reputation for integrity. Programs like "Worn Wear" go even further, encouraging customers to repair and reuse their gear instead of replacing it, reducing waste, and showcasing Patagonia's dedication to sustainability.

In 2022, Patagonia elevated its environmental mission to new heights by pledging all profits to fight climate change and support conservation efforts. This groundbreaking decision resonated deeply with its audience and solidified the company's position as a corporate responsibility leader. Instead of following the traditional marketing playbook, Patagonia relies on community-driven content and authentic brand ambassadors who embody its values. By avoiding influencer-heavy campaigns, the brand appeals to consumers who prioritize sincerity over slick promotions.

. . .

PATAGONIA'S NUMBERS tell a powerful story of its impact and growth. In 2023, its eCommerce sales reached approximately $422 million globally, reflecting the growing product demand. While Patagonia remains privately held and doesn't frequently share detailed financials, analysts estimate the company's annual revenue has surpassed $1 billion. This remarkable growth underscores the brand's influence in the outdoor apparel industry and its ability to combine profitability with purpose.

BECOMING ESSENTIAL FACTOR: Inspirational Values

PATAGONIA CULTIVATES deep customer loyalty by putting environmental and social responsibility at the heart of its business. The company's mission to "save our home planet" shapes every aspect of its operations, creating a brand identity that resonates powerfully with ethically minded consumers. Patagonia doesn't just talk about sustainability; it integrates this mission into its actions. The company consistently donates 1% of its sales to environmental causes, and it goes a step further with its "Worn Wear" program. These practices demonstrate a commitment to reducing waste and promoting conscious consumption, earning the trust and admiration of a growing customer base.

Patagonia's activism further strengthens its bond with customers. The company has taken bold steps to protect public lands, even engaging in high-profile lawsuits, and actively advocates for climate change legislation. By taking these stances, Patagonia positions itself as a brand willing to take charge of critical global issues. It aligns with customers who want to support businesses that prioritize purpose over profit. This alignment has created a loyal community of customers who see their purchases as part of a broader commitment to environmental stewardship.

The company's continued success is deeply rooted in its unwavering commitment to sustainability and ethical practices. Patagonia's high-quality products reflect its values, blending functionality, durability, and environmental responsibility. Customers return for the reliability of its gear and because they trust the brand to uphold principles they care about. This unique combination of advocacy and product excellence has made Patagonia a revenue and customer loyalty leader.

Across generations, Patagonia's message of responsibility and its genuine efforts to make a difference have resonated deeply. It has become more than an outdoor apparel company—a movement for change. By staying true to its values, Patagonia proves that businesses can thrive while making a meaningful impact, inspiring customers to join them in their mission to protect the planet. This commitment to purpose has solidified Patagonia's status as a trailblazer in sustainability and a beloved brand for consumers who want their purchases to reflect their principles.

LEARNINGS

HOW TO MAKE it work in your offering:

- Key Customer Driver: A stimulating, inspirational story.
    - Storytelling is different from a story of values. One refers to a narrative, like a brand highlighting victories, versus a brand with authentic social commitment and support to relevant causes. A brand with values focuses on the "why" behind actions and decisions.

- What to Identify: Customer/Brand synchronic values.
    - The zeitgeist or spirit of our times emphasizes digital connectivity, environmental consciousness, and recognition of diversity and social equity. Keeping current society's emerging values is the first step any brand should take to strategize what will be its ownable "why."

- "Essential" Insert: A touching, personal component.
    - Societal values are essential, but we can't exclude what can land all of them on a personal level. Two examples: Microsoft's focus on diversity, inclusion, and accessibility, especially with initiatives like the development of the Xbox Adaptive Controller for gamers with disabilities, aligns with societal efforts to make technology accessible

to everyone. The second example Chipotle connects its commitment to ethical sourcing and sustainable food practices with the personal values of customers who care about where their food comes from and how it impacts the environment.

- Key Customer Reward: Becoming a caring agent of change.
  - A brand becoming responsible for more than its product typically happens when it extends its influence to broader societal, environmental, or ethical concerns. This transition involves the brand aligning with values beyond simply delivering goods or services. As a result, the brand often becomes a part of more significant movements or societal conversations, and its responsibility expands to include its impact on communities, ecosystems, and global issues.

- Brand Becomes: Feel-good commitment.
  - A brand can become a "feel-good" brand by cultivating a reputation that resonates emotionally with consumers, making them feel connected, positive, and even proud to support it. Emotional tattoos are the invisible but powerful emotional connections brands or experiences create with individuals,

leaving a long-lasting imprint on their identity, behavior, and decision-making.

IN SUMMARY:

YOU WILL UPGRADE your offering from "interesting" to an "emotional alignment."

7

Becoming Essential Way #7: Get the Right Code

Foundation

The Model or Theory Behind It

THE CODE REFLECTS the unconscious meanings we attach to things like cars, food, relationships, or even countries, shaped by the culture we grew up in. Think of the code as a key that unlocks the gap between what people say and what they actually do. In this gap sits what they truly mean. To unlock it, you must understand the deeper reasons behind choosing a product or service and the hidden context. A well-understood code gives you a more precise, macro view of the cultural context—like putting on corrective lenses—and helps you pinpoint the right insights.

CULTURAL CODES OFFER a fascinating way to understand how people in different societies interpret the world. They work like a hidden language—a set of shared, often unspoken meanings and associations that people in a culture apply to objects, behaviors, or ideas. These meanings go beyond what's visible on the surface and tap into collective emotional and psychological connections developed over time. The concept of cultural codes gained attention from theorists and marketers who noticed that although people may seem to react to things based on personal preference, deep-rooted cultural patterns often shape their choices and behaviors in predictable ways.

Take food as an example. In one culture, a particular dish might symbolize comfort, warmth, and family bonding because people traditionally serve it at family gatherings. The same dish might have no meaning or even seem strange or unappetizing in another culture. Each culture attaches meaning to food based on historical experiences, rituals, and social contexts. For instance, in the United States, people often associate apple pie with home, tradition, and national identity. In other cultures, however, it might be seen as a dessert with no particular cultural significance.

Cultural codes go beyond food; they shape how we view and respond to fashion, technology, and even abstract ideas like time and success. For example, in Western societies, cars often represent freedom and individualism, reflecting a culture that values independence. In contrast, in countries with efficient public transportation, people may view cars as a symbol of luxury or social status rather than personal freedom. These differences arise from the unique historical and social conditions that shape each society's values.

The theory behind cultural codes suggests that people absorb these meanings unconsciously as they grow up in their environment, families, and communities. This process starts in early childhood and becomes deeply ingrained as they grow. By adulthood, they may not realize these codes are at work; they just feel "right" or "wrong" without questioning why.

Relevance

Marketers, advertisers, and anthropologists are deeply interested in cultural codes because they are potent tools for forming solid and authentic connections with audiences. By understanding these codes, businesses can tap into a broad range of emotional and cultural associations, crafting messages or product images that resonate with people on a deeply subconscious level. This connection is vital for influencing consumer behavior, as it allows brands to align themselves with their audience's core values and beliefs without needing to state them explicitly. A successful advertising campaign, for example, will use these cultural codes to subtly communicate a message that speaks to the audience's unspoken truths, making the product feel inherently relevant and desirable. Iconic examples like Nike's "Just Do It," Apple's "Think Different," and L'Oréal's "Because You're Worth It" demonstrate how powerful these codes can be in shaping consumer perception and creating lasting emotional engagement with the brand.

On a broader level, understanding cultural codes is essential for effective cross-cultural communication. Different cultures come with codes, leading to misunderstandings or conflicts when people from diverse backgrounds interact. For example, the same gesture, word, or object can have different meanings in different cultures. Without recognizing these subtle but significant differences, people may misinterpret each other's actions or intentions, leading to confusion or tension. By becoming aware of these cultural nuances, individuals can develop greater empathy and open-mindedness. This awareness encourages a more thoughtful approach to interaction that looks beyond superficial differences and seeks to understand the underlying cultural frameworks that shape each person's worldview. This shift in perspective helps foster more respectful and meaningful conversations between individuals from different cultural backgrounds.

It's important to clarify that cultural codes are not the strategy or the critical insight behind a marketing campaign. Instead, they represent a long-term, macro-level view of the cultural landscape surrounding a category or product. They help marketers see the bigger picture, uncovering patterns and connections that might otherwise remain hidden. This broader perspective allows brands to position themselves in a way that feels intuitive and authentic to their audience. In many ways, cultural codes are the key to unlocking the "Aha! Moment" for marketers and consumers—offering a deeper understanding of the emotional and psychological triggers that drive consumer behavior.

Think of it like the Rosetta Stone, used to decode ancient Egyptian hieroglyphics. Just as that tool unlocked the meaning behind a complex and obscure language, cultural codes help marketers decode the cultural messages that resonate most deeply with their audience.

. . .

AT THE *EMPATHY* LEVEL, the following psychological motivations are crucial to understand and cater to:

- **Vitality:** The most critical umbrella motivation.

- Primal
- Unconscious
- Sensibility
- Uplifting
- Comprehensive

RELATED MARKETING CONCEPTS ARE:

- Interconnected
- Whole
- Intimate
- Vibrant
- Uncovering

CASE EXAMPLE
Airbnb

BACKGROUND

In 2007, two roommates, Brian Chesky and Joe Gebbia, struggled with high rent in San Francisco. Rather than simply looking for a cheaper place, they decided to get creative and turned their apartment into a small bed-and-breakfast, offering guests an air mattress and breakfast. To make it all work, they created a website called AirBed & Breakfast, targeting travelers looking for affordable, short-term places to stay, especially during significant events like conventions when hotels were fully booked. By 2008, they brought in Nathan Blecharczyk as their third co-founder and officially launched Airbnb at the SXSW festival in Austin. Though the site initially had trouble attracting users, the founders didn't give up. They found creative ways to fund the business, including selling election-themed cereal in 2008. Their big break came when Y Combinator invested in them, providing the support they needed to grow, build a user base, and fine-tune the platform.

AIRBNB'S SUCCESS came from tapping into the correct cultural code and understanding how modern travelers' needs and values were changing. The company appealed to a growing desire for more personalized, authentic experiences rather than the typical hotel stay. This insight perfectly fits the broader cultural trend of valuing experiences over material possessions. Airbnb positioned itself as a way for people to "belong anywhere," making it not just about finding a place to stay but about offering an experience that felt more connected and personal.

FROM THE START, Airbnb recognized the power of community—both for hosts and guests—and worked to create an environment built on trust and connection. Airbnb's focus on human experiences, not just on providing lodging, matched a growing interest in exploring local cultures and unique spaces. The platform also understood the importance of user-generated content. Guest reviews and ratings became crucial for establishing social proof, helping to build trust and credibility for the platform, and further fueling its growth.

PERFORMANCE

AIRBNB'S GROWTH has been impressive, marked by significant milestones in terms of users, listings, and market value. When the company started in 2008, it was just three co-founders with fewer than 100 listings. However, in 09, Airbnb expanded quickly, reaching over 2,500 listings across ten countries. By 2011, the platform had made huge strides, spreading to over 89 countries and booking more than 1 million nights worldwide. The following year, in 2012, Airbnb celebrated hosting tents with ten million guests, a massive sign of its growing popularity.

THE RAPID EXPANSION didn't stop there. In 2014, Airbnb reached a $10 billion valuation, and by 2015, it had hosted 17 million guests and amassed 2 million listings across the globe. By 2016, Airbnb was celebrating another major milestone: 100 million guest arrivals. A year later, in 2017, the company reached 4 million listings in more than 191 countries, further cementing its place as a leader in the travel industry.

. . .

FINANCIALLY, Airbnb's growth trajectory continued to skyrocket, reaching a $31 billion valuation in 2019 after a successful funding round. Then came the challenges of the pandemic in 2020, which disrupted the travel industry as a whole. However, despite the setbacks, Airbnb remained resilient. That year, it generated $3.4 billion in revenue and became profitable for the first time. That same year, Airbnb went public with an IPO valuation of $47 billion. By 2021, the company's valuation had exploded to over $100 billion, a testament to how far it had come from those early days in a San Francisco apartment.

BECOMING ESSENTIAL FACTOR: Customized Experience

AS OF 2024, Airbnb has grown to an impressive 6 million listings across more than 220 countries and regions, with over 1 billion guest arrivals. The platform didn't stop at just offering places to stay—it expanded its services to include Airbnb Experiences, where locals host unique activities, adding another layer to its influence in the travel and lodging world. This move helped Airbnb further solidify its presence as a place for short-term stays and a complete travel experience.

BY TAPPING into changing values and leveraging technology to build trust and create connections, Airbnb didn't just become an alternative to traditional hotels. It symbolized a new way of thinking about travel and hospitality, reflecting a shift toward more personal, authentic experiences. This shift played a massive role in making Airbnb the cultural icon it is today. It's not just about finding a place to sleep—it's about discovering new places, new experiences, and new ways to connect with the world.

Learnings

How to make it work in your offering:

- Key Customer Driver: Vitality. Aliveness
    - A brand becomes vital when it creates a unique experience or offers something customers can't easily find elsewhere. This vitality could be convenience, exclusivity, or a product that genuinely improves the customer's life in a way competitors don't. When customers start to view the brand as essential, they don't just buy from it—they advocate for it, integrate it into their lives, and often remain loyal for years, which involves the brand staying relevant and unchallenged.

- What to Identify: The unspoken, unconscious thread.
    - The Holy Grail of brand embedment happens when it becomes so deeply

ingrained in a customer's life, experiences, and identity that their loyalty to it becomes almost unconscious. It's not just about choosing to buy a product; it's about creating a connection so strong that the customer doesn't even think twice about their preference. Over time, a brand should be able to identify customer's values and experiences that help it to become intertwined with their habits, emotions, and worldview, making the brand a natural and indispensable part of their life.

- "Essential" Insert: Intimate understanding
    - Showing how much your brand cares for its customers involves constant caring and attention to detail. Personalized experiences or anticipating needs exemplify how the brand listens to its users. Chewy, the online pet supplier retailer, among other proactive initiatives, doesn't just wait for customers to reach out with problems. The company is proactive, checking in on customers with follow-up emails after significant purchases, like medications or new pet products. They also monitor customer accounts and send reminders when pet food or other supplies are running low, making it easier for customers to restock without thinking about it.

. . .

- Key Customer Reward: Uplifting empathy
    - Brands can achieve the highest level of empathy by looking at the category from its user's point of view. For instance, Fitbit understands its customers by tapping into their growing desire for health and wellness tracking. By allowing users to monitor their physical activity, sleep patterns, and overall fitness goals, Fitbit doesn't just offer a product—it helps customers achieve personal well-being. The integration with an app that tracks progress, gives tips, and provides motivation shows that Fitbit understands its users' desire to improve their health and stay on track.

- Brand Becomes: Independence
    - Independence happens when a brand gets the correct code and gives its customers a sense of autonomy, like renting through Airbnb, crafting with Etsy, or developing websites with GoDaddy. These brands foster independence by offering tools, services, and products that allow customers to take control of their decisions, experiences, and outcomes, aligning with their personal preferences and values.

In summary:

You will upgrade your offering from "knowing" to "understanding."

8

Becoming Essential Way #8: Make It Easy

Foundation

The Model or Theory Behind It

Easy is easy: sugar, a warm Sunday, summer, and recess. It instantly takes us back to places we love, just like the states of mind we want to re-live. That's why we keep watching the same shows or movies—they're like a jukebox for our moods.

Easy connects naturally with the pleasure centers of our brain, closer to sweet than sour. It taps into our inner child, helping us ultimately focus on whatever we're into. It makes us lose track of time, ourselves, and our problems. A crucial part of Easy is the instant reward, plus the bonus of making us feel competent.

Mihaly Csikszentmihalyi's theory of flow explains this state. Csikszentmihalyi, a psychologist at the University of Chicago, found that when people are in flow, they get so absorbed in what they're doing that they lose track of time, their surroundings, and even themselves. It's not just about deep focus; it's a rewarding, productive experience that makes tasks exciting and fulfilling. When in flow, people feel purposeful and engaged, which leads to better productivity, creativity, and satisfaction.

The trick to getting into flow is finding the balance between your skills and the task's challenge. If the challenge is too much, you'll feel anxious or overwhelmed. If it's too easy, you'll get bored or disengaged. Flow happens when the task is challenging but doable, stretching your abilities just enough to keep you in the zone where you're motivated and focused.

In this state, everything clicks. You're not distracted by random thoughts or outside events. Your mind and body are in sync, making actions feel smooth and effortless. Time flies unnoticed, and you're in a blissful zone of energized concentration, where everything flows from one task to the next without pause.

Flow is more than just fun; it is excellent for learning and growth. Whenever you experience it, you're working at the top of your abilities, pushing just a little past your limits. This stretching helps you improve and grow to take on bigger, more challenging goals. Over time, flow enables you to keep getting better as higher skill levels push you to embrace even more ambitious challenges.

Flow also boosts mental well-being. It keeps you focused on the present, making it a natural form of mindfulness. It reduces stress and prevents overthinking or worrying. Flow brings you a sense of purpose, satisfaction, and self-worth. It enriches your work and your life as you find deeper meaning in what you do.

In short, Csikszentmihalyi's flow theory shows that balancing skills with challenges creates the ideal space for deep focus, pleasure, and growth. Flow is available to anyone willing to challenge themselves, making it a valuable tool for improving personal and professional experiences.

Relevance

Flow significantly impacts marketing by showing how to create experiences that grab consumers' attention and build strong brand loyalty. When brands design products, experiences, or environments that help people get into a flow state, they boost engagement and create deeper emotional connections. In marketing, flow is about crafting interactions that pull consumers into a fun, immersive experience, keeping them engaged longer and leaving them with a positive, lasting impression of the brand.

FLOW IS critical in digital marketing. Good websites, apps, or platforms offer a smooth, intuitive experience that lets users easily browse content or products. By eliminating obstacles and making the design feel effortless to navigate, brands can keep users hooked, encouraging them to stick around longer and connect more with the brand. When someone hits flow while using a website or app, they're more likely to interact meaningfully—watching a video, reading an article, or making a purchase—because the experience feels rewarding.

FLOW ALSO SHINES IN GAMIFICATION, which applies game-like elements to non-gaming settings. Marketers can create experiences that keep consumers engaged and invested by adding challenges, achievements, and rewards. Flow happens when the challenge matches the consumer's skill level, motivating them to dive fully into the experience. Take fitness apps, for example—these apps use challenges and rewards to keep users engaged. They encourage long-term commitment and brand loyalty by letting users track their progress, earn rewards, and set new goals. Users keep returning because the app offers just enough challenges to stay engaging while helping them master things at their own pace.

ADVERTISING CAMPAIGNS CAN ALSO TAP into flow by creating stories or interactive elements that grab the viewer's attention and strengthen their connection to the message. When an ad tells a compelling story or presents a challenge that aligns with the viewer's needs, it keeps them engaged and encourages active participation. A user fully immersed in a message is likelier to remember the brand and act on the call to action.

FLOW IS critical to marketing because it connects brand engagement with consumer satisfaction. By designing seamless, enjoyable, and stimulating experiences that captivate and keep users immersed, brands can build loyalty and emotional attachment—critical in today's competitive market. Flow principles help marketers create experiences that pull consumers in and keep them returning, turning casual interest into a lasting commitment.

AT THE *SIMPLICITY* LEVEL, the following psychological motivations are crucial to understand and cater to:

- **Stimulation:** The most critical umbrella motivation.

- Reward
- Command
- Harmony
- Joy
- Satisfaction

RELATED MARKETING CONCEPTS ARE:

- The feeling of competence.
- Pride
- Focus
- Frictionless
- Seamless
- Excitement

CASE EXAMPLE
Uber

BACKGROUND

Uber was founded in 2009 by Garrett Camp, co-founder of StumbleUpon, and Travis Kalanick, a tech entrepreneur. They wanted to solve the problem of finding reliable transportation, especially when things get busy. Camp had the idea one snowy evening in Paris when he struggled to find a cab. He envisioned a service that would let people book rides easily through a mobile app. At first, they called the company UberCab, focusing on providing an alternative to traditional taxis.

Uber kicked off its first test run in San Francisco in 2010, offering premium black car services that users could order with just a few taps on their smartphones. The app took off because it was simple and reliable. By 2011, Uber expanded to other major U.S. cities and attracted significant venture capital funding, which helped it grow into a global brand. In 2012, Uber launched UberX, a cheaper option allowing almost anyone with a car to become a driver. This initiative was a game-changer, disrupting the transportation industry by offering more affordable rides and creating new income opportunities for people.

As the company grew, it ran into regulatory hurdles, competition from local taxi services, and legal challenges worldwide. Uber's rapid growth and some controversial business practices made it one of the most high-profile startups ever. In 2017, after facing criticism over corporate culture and Kalanick's leadership, Kalanick stepped down as CEO, and Dara Khosrowshahi took over.

Under Khosrowshahi, Uber cleaned up its image and focused on long-term growth. The company branched into new areas, such as food delivery with Uber Eats, freight logistics with Uber Freight, and other mobility solutions. In 2019, Uber went public, marking a significant milestone. Since then, the company has continued to evolve, investing in technology, sustainability, and partnerships to improve urban mobility.

Today, Uber operates in hundreds of cities worldwide, connecting riders with drivers through its app and offering various transportation and delivery services. Its journey has transformed Uber from a disruptive startup into a global tech giant, completely changing the ride-hailing and transportation game.

Performance

Uber has grown incredibly fast since it started in 2009. It kicked off in San Francisco in 2010, and by 2011, it had expanded to New York City and Paris. By 2013, it was in 35 cities around the world. This rapid growth attracted significant venture capital, and by 2018, Uber had raised about $11.5 billion. In 2015, its valuation hit $51 billion; by the time it went public in 2019, it was worth around $75 billion. The IPO raised $8.1 billion, with an initial market cap of $82.4 billion. By 2022, Uber's revenue soared to $31.9 billion, up from $11.1 billion in 2020, showing a solid rebound and growth, mainly thanks to Uber Eats.

Today, Uber serves over 130 million active users worldwide, has over 5 million drivers, and operates in over 900 cities across 70+ countries. In 2018, Uber hit the milestone of 10 billion trips. Uber Eats, launched in 2014, has become a significant revenue stream, pulling in $10.9 billion in 2022, making it one of the top global food delivery services. These numbers prove Uber's ability to scale, diversify, and maintain its position as the global mobility and delivery services leader.

Becoming Essential Factor: Seamless Transaction

Uber leverages the concepts of flow, frictionlessness, and ease to create a seamless user experience that enhances customer satisfaction and loyalty. The Uber app's design emphasizes simplicity and removes obstacles from the ride-booking process, allowing users to access transportation quickly without stress. By focusing on an interface that requires minimal effort, Uber keeps users in a flow state, guiding them from opening the app to booking a ride in just a few taps. This streamlined experience keeps users engaged by minimizing distractions and simplifying each step, from selecting the destination to tracking the driver's arrival.

Uber also applies frictionless design to its payment and rating systems. Users don't need to worry about cash or complicated payment methods because the app processes transactions automatically, providing a smooth experience from start to finish. After the ride, Uber encourages an intuitive and fast rating and feedback process. This enables riders and drivers to maintain the flow without unnecessary delays.

Furthermore, Uber's use of predictive algorithms for ride matching and estimated arrival times contributes to ease and convenience. The app uses real-time data to anticipate demand, adjust pricing, and provide accurate ETAs, reducing the cognitive load on users who otherwise might have to wait or calculate arrival times. This efficient, responsive system helps users feel in control and reduces the mental stress of worrying about timing or availability.

By prioritizing flow, frictionlessness, and ease, Uber fosters a positive, reliable user experience that keeps customers engaged and minimizes the steps they must take. Thus, Uber is not just a transportation service but an integral part of users' everyday routines.

LEARNINGS

How to make it work in your offering:

- Key Customer Driver: Stimulation
    - In today's world, every brand has to adapt to the expectations set by the digital age, where we demand quick, constant, and personalized experiences. People are used to instant gratification, and brands must respond in real time, whether through fast customer service, quick content updates, or efficient delivery services. Customers will quickly look elsewhere if a brand doesn't meet these expectations.

- What to Identify: Inner-child motivations.
  - The dynamic nature of digital experiences also means that brands need to keep evolving. Just offering static products or services isn't enough anymore. Brands must engage customers with new content, fresh offers, and constantly updated experiences to keep them returning.

- "Essential" Insert: Sleek and simple.
  - In the digital age, where attention is scarce and time is limited, sleek and straightforward brands cater to our desire for efficiency, clarity, and ease—qualities that have become essential in a fast-moving, tech-heavy world. Muji is a Japanese retailer that's all about sleekness and simplicity. The brand's design products have a minimalist philosophy—nothing flashy, just well-made, functional items that look sleek and stylish without being overdone. The brand's stores and marketing create a calming, clutter-free environment, reinforcing their focus on simplicity. Dyson has revolutionized home appliances, giving customers the tools to master cleanliness and efficiency with sleek, high-tech designs.

- Key Customer Reward: Mastery

- Mastery captures the sense of having complete control, expertise, and confidence in navigating the complexities of modern life. In a world that demands constant adaptation to new technologies, evolving expectations, and fast-paced changes, mastery represents thriving, a deep understanding, and skill in managing diverse aspects of life. Mastery instills a sense of pride and accomplishment, showing competence.

- Brand Becomes: A reward
  - A brand that simplifies the digital experience or enhances personal productivity doesn't just offer a product—it gives customers the tools to feel like they've mastered their environment. This benefit taps into their desire for competence, control, and efficiency. The brand becomes a badge of achievement, as customers associate their use of it with their ability to handle the demands of the modern world. Some brand examples:
    - T-Mobile – Simplifying mobile plans and communication, giving users the tools to master connectivity with flexible, user-centric services.
    - Square – Making payments simple and accessible for small businesses, helping entrepreneurs master financial transactions and growth.

- Coursera – Offering accessible online learning, helping users master new skills and advance their knowledge from anywhere.

IN SUMMARY:

YOU WILL UPGRADE your offering from "simple" to "a rewarding tool."

9

Becoming Essential Way #9: Facilitate Connectivity

Foundation

The Model or Theory Behind It

CONNECTIVITY EXPANDS REACH and builds social links, helping relationships flourish between a brand, its users, and the broader community. It transforms a brand into a portal where customers explore more about the brand or category and a blank canvas where users post, share, and create. By doing so, connectivity combats the isolation many feel today, unlocking the innate power of communication—a primal, sensory drive. The richer the experience, the deeper the connection.

At its essence, connectivity theory examines how relationships, networks, and interactions drive the flow of information, influence, and resources. It maps pathways linking individuals or groups, enabling ideas, energy, and support to move freely. Rooted in systems thinking, the science of understanding how things interact within a larger whole, connectivity theory views each connection as part of an intricate web where a single change can ripple through the entire network.

The theory argues that network structure and density shape outcomes: More connections mean greater access to diverse resources and knowledge. Online networks exemplify this, as connectivity spreads information instantly and supports collective problem-solving. Strong networks foster resilience, allowing them to adapt more effectively to disruptions.

Connectivity theory shows how networks amplify individual actions. A single effort can ripple through connections, sparking exponential changes. In social networks, one influencer's message might cascade across their followers, shifting norms or triggering movements. Influence and information travel through these connections, making network structure pivotal in determining impact.

The connectivity theory stresses the value of open communication and collaborative systems in organizations. Well-connected teams innovate faster, blending diverse ideas into more robust solutions. In contrast, isolated teams or individuals slow progress and limit opportunities. This understanding has driven a focus on fostering collaboration across departments and roles in modern businesses.

In ecosystems, connectivity theory highlights the interdependence of species and environmental factors. Changes in one area affect the whole, showing how biodiversity strengthens resilience. When species lose connections, ecosystems risk collapse. Similarly, urban planners use connectivity principles to design integrated transit systems and green spaces, improving mobility, access, and quality of life.

Connectivity binds us, shaping behaviors, opportunities, and systems while strengthening the networks that sustain our world.

Relevancy

Digital connectivity has accelerated this transformation, creating global networks that cross traditional boundaries and reshape economies, cultures, and social structures. It has also changed how humans interact, offering benefits like increased collaboration and instant access to information while introducing challenges such as privacy risks and information overload. This duality highlights a paradox: while modern networks empower and unite us, they also create complexities and dangers that demand careful management.

Connectivity theory reveals the patterns and effects of these networks across different areas. It offers a way to understand how interconnected systems evolve, adapt, or fail. As network science and technology advance, the theory provides fresh insights into how enhancing or controlling connectivity impacts personal, social, and environmental outcomes.

During the pandemic, digital connectivity became a lifeline. It helped people maintain relationships, work remotely, and access vital information and services, bridging the gap created by physical isolation. Virtual collaboration, online education, and telemedicine transformed how society functioned under lockdowns and restrictions. This connectivity proved crucial, enabling individuals, businesses, and communities to adapt, stay informed, and keep moving forward in the face of unprecedented challenges.

At the *enabling* level, the following psychological motivations are crucial to understand and cater to:

- **Connection:** The most critical umbrella motivation.

- Creation
- Empowerment
- Control
- Self-esteem
- Community

Related marketing concepts are:

- Having a voice.
- Conversation enabler
- Personal spaces
- Reaching out
- Expanding reach

Case Example

Zoom

BACKGROUND

Zoom's journey began in 2011 when Eric Yuan, an engineer and Cisco vice president, set out to create a better video conferencing solution. After leading WebEx, Cisco's platform, Yuan saw repeated usability, quality, and scalability issues that frustrated users. Determined to build a more intuitive and effective tool, he left Cisco and launched Zoom Video Communications. Yuan envisioned a platform that would allow people to connect effortlessly, free from the technical hiccups of existing tools.

In 2013, Zoom debuted its first product, Zoom Meetings, positioning itself as a high-quality, reliable option for video communication. Offering HD video and audio, support for large group meetings, and compatibility across devices, Zoom stood out for its simplicity and consistency. Early adopters in business, education, and small-to-medium enterprises embraced the platform. Yuan's strategy of offering free access with a 40-minute limit fueled rapid growth, allowing individuals and small teams to connect without cost while encouraging larger organizations to invest in premium plans with advanced features.

Over the years, Zoom expanded its offerings, introducing tools like Zoom Rooms for conference room integration and Zoom Webinars for virtual events. By prioritizing video quality, user-friendly design, and continual feature updates, Zoom gained significant traction, especially in the corporate and educational sectors. By 2017, Zoom achieved "unicorn" status with a valuation exceeding $1 billion, cementing its place as a tech industry leader. Yuan's commitment to customer feedback kept Zoom ahead of competitors, as the company consistently rolled out user-requested features.

Zoom went public in April 2019 with one of the year's standout IPOs, showcasing solid financial performance. In early 2020, the COVID-19 pandemic catapulted Zoom into the global spotlight. With remote work, education, healthcare, and social interactions suddenly dependent on virtual communication, Zoom became indispensable. Downloads soared as millions turned to the platform to stay connected during lockdowns.

Zoom's explosive growth came with challenges. It faced scrutiny over privacy and security, including incidents of unauthorized users' "Zoombombing" meetings. Yuan and his team acted swiftly, implementing end-to-end encryption, waiting rooms, and more robust authentication measures to address vulnerabilities. These upgrades reassured users and helped Zoom maintain its dominance despite rising competition from platforms like Microsoft Teams and Google Meet.

Zoom continues to evolve post-pandemic. New features like Zoom Apps and Events expand its functionality beyond traditional meetings. Yuan's vision of seamless, accessible connectivity has made Zoom a household name, revolutionizing how people work, learn, and stay connected remotely.

Performance

Zoom's user growth and revenue took off, especially after 2019. In its first year as a public company, it reported $622 million in revenue—a 78% jump from the previous year. By early 2020, as the COVID-19 pandemic forced the world to adopt remote communication, Zoom's daily meeting participants skyrocketed from 10 million in December 2019 to over 300 million by April 2020.

BECOMING ESSENTIAL

. . .

THIS METEORIC RISE brought financial success. For the fiscal year ending January 2021, Zoom's revenue soared to $2.65 billion, a staggering 326% year-over-year increase. Net income followed suit, jumping from $21.7 million in 2019 to $671.5 million in 2021. The company also saw a 470% spike in customers, generating over $100,000 annually, highlighting its growing appeal among significant enterprises and organizations.

ZOOM'S stock price reflected this surge, climbing from around $60 at its IPO in April 2019 to over $500 at its peak in late 2020. Even as remote work tapered off in 2021, Zoom remained dominant. By fiscal year 2022, revenue hit $4.1 billion, marking a 55% increase. Its user base continued expanding across industries, from corporations to schools, healthcare providers, and even entertainment, where virtual experiences thrived.

THE PLATFORM'S usage metrics also underscored its dominance. By 2021, Zoom handled up to 3.5 trillion annual meeting minutes, with users logging billions of minutes daily as hybrid work models became standard. By 2022, over 500,000 businesses had signed on as paying customers, cementing Zoom's role in enterprise communication.

These numbers capture Zoom's evolution into a top-tier digital communication platform. Eric Yuan's dedication to user experience and adaptability allowed the company to scale rapidly, meeting the demands of a world relying on virtual connectivity. During this transformative period,

Zoom became a cornerstone of communication technology for businesses and communities worldwide.

BECOMING ESSENTIAL FACTOR: Enabling Connectivity

ZOOM BECAME indispensable by positioning itself as a powerful tool for connectivity. It offered seamless, accessible, and reliable video communication that kept people connected across distances. During the COVID-19 pandemic, its user-friendly design, flexibility, and high-quality performance quickly made it the go-to platform for anyone needing a stable way to communicate remotely. Zoom stood out by effortlessly scaling to meet the massive surge in demand for remote work, online education, telemedicine, and virtual social gatherings.

ZOOM BRIDGED physical divides as a connectivity enabler with a simple and intuitive setup. Users could join or host meetings with just a few clicks, bypassing the technical hurdles that frustrated other platforms. Its compatibility across devices—smartphones, tablets, and computers—made it accessible to a broad audience. This inclusivity allowed millions worldwide to easily integrate Zoom into their lives without special tools or expertise.

ZOOM ENSURED CONTINUITY FOR BUSINESSES, transforming their operations. Organizations adopted it to keep teams connected, foster collaboration, and maintain productivity in remote settings. From one-on-one check-ins to large-scale webinars, Zoom has adapted to the needs of small businesses and global corporations. As hybrid work became desirable, Zoom cemented its role as an essential part of the modern workplace, supporting a seamless blend of in-person and virtual interactions.

ZOOM'S impact went far beyond the corporate world. Schools and universities turned to Zoom to run virtual classes, ensuring education continued uninterrupted during lockdowns. Teachers and students embraced features like screen sharing and breakout rooms to recreate the classroom experience online. In healthcare, Zoom enabled telemedicine, allowing doctors and patients to connect remotely and maintain care despite restrictions on physical visits. Even social events—family gatherings, religious services, and weddings—moved onto Zoom, helping people sustain relationships and celebrate milestones despite isolation.

THIS VERSATILITY MADE Zoom more than just a product; it became critical infrastructure at a time when connection mattered most. Its rapid response to user needs, including rolling out security upgrades and simplifying features, reinforced its reputation as a reliable platform. By consistently improving and meeting diverse connectivity demands, Zoom proved how a trusted connectivity enabler could transform how people interact, work, learn, and socialize across distances.

LEARNINGS

How to make it work in your offering:

- Key Customer Driver: Connectivity
  - There are many "flavors" of how brands enable and engage users in connectivity. Here are some examples:
    - Connecting Products: P&G's Herbal Essences for Teens uses playful, interactive packaging that encourages engagement. Their shampoo and conditioner bottle designs fit like puzzle pieces, with their shapes and graphics aligning when placed side by side to form a complete image or message. This creative approach adds a fun element to the product, appealing to younger users and making the bottles visually stand out on shelves. It also subtly promotes buying both products together as a set, enhancing brand cohesion and boosting sales.
    - Connecting Professionals: LinkedIn excels at connecting people by focusing entirely on professional networking. Unlike other social platforms, it creates meaningful connections based on careers, skills, and shared goals. Each profile acts as a digital résumé, showcasing work history, certifications, and endorsements, making it easy for users to represent

themselves professionally.
  - Creating Ecosystems: Apple makes a tightly integrated ecosystem with devices like the iPhone, iPad, Mac, and Apple Watch, all connected through services like Apple One and iCloud and apps like Apple Music and FaceTime. This connectivity encourages loyalty and convenience as users effortlessly transition between devices.

- What to Identify: Customer and social network expectations.
  - Today, people expect to stay connected effortlessly, no matter where or what they do. Whether it's a quick message to a friend, a virtual meeting with coworkers, or streaming a favorite show, they want everything to work smoothly and without frustration. It's not just about technology—it's about feeling close to others, even when apart. Users look for tools that make communication natural, like hopping between devices without losing a beat or seeing loved ones' faces crystal clear on a video call. More than anything, people expect these connections to feel real, helping them share, collaborate, and belong.

- "Essential" Insert: People's exchanges facilitator.

- A brand can enhance people's connectivity by creating experiences that feel natural, seamless, and meaningful. It starts with understanding how people interact and what they value most in staying connected, whether through technology, community, or shared experiences. Brands should offer intuitive tools or platforms that remove barriers to interaction. By doing so, brands can make it easier for people to communicate, collaborate, and build relationships.

- Key Customer Reward: Having a voice.
  - Customers want to feel heard and valued, so they seek meaningful opportunities to engage with brands. They look for platforms where they can share feedback, ideas, and opinions and where their voices directly impact decisions and experiences. For example, Starbucks' "My Starbucks Idea" platform allows customers to suggest and vote on product ideas, leading to popular menu additions like the Pumpkin Cream Cold Brew. Similarly, LEGO Ideas invites fans to submit designs for new LEGO sets, and successful entries go into production.

- Brand Becomes: An Enabler.

- A brand becomes an enabler by removing obstacles and making things more accessible. It's not just about releasing a product, service, or platform; it's about understanding customers' needs and providing tools or experiences that make their lives easier.

IN SUMMARY:

YOU WILL UPGRADE your offering from "a connector" to "a catalyst."

10

Becoming Essential Way #10: Emphasize the Authentic

Foundation

The Model or Theory Behind It

As the world grows more artificial, individual and social cravings for authenticity intensify. In this new reality of "reality TV," celebrities, influencers, and AI avatars, your brand voice expresses what you stand for, adding depth and meaning.

There are many ways to be authentic:

- Natural authenticity: This way is about being honest and trustworthy about your values—

using simple, honest ingredients or methods and being upfront about where stuff comes from. It's about doing the right thing for the planet and people without the fluff or greenwashing. Seventh Generation makes everyday cleaning products safer for us and the earth. They use non-toxic, biodegradable ingredients and eco-friendly packaging, focusing on sustainability. They're transparent about what's in their products and push for more robust environmental policies. This brand covers you if you care about the earth and your health.

- Original authenticity: The first of its kind (new or old). Original authenticity is about a brand being authentic to itself, staying genuine, and not pretending to be something it's not. It's about sticking to your core values and being authentic in everything you do. For over a century, Crayola has embodied original authenticity through its unwavering commitment to creativity, learning, and self-expression. The brand has become synonymous with childhood imagination, evoking nostalgia for generations while remaining a cornerstone of art supplies in classrooms and homes.

- Referential authenticity: This way is about creating real, meaningful experiences that align with a brand's values and connect with people on a deeper level. It's not just about selling a product but about making customers feel something genuine through the experience, whether through personal interactions, storytelling, or immersive events. Harley-Davidson creates

experiential authenticity by offering riders more than just motorcycles—it's about the feeling of freedom and rebellion. The brand connects deeply with people's lifestyles through events like the Sturgis Motorcycle Rally and a strong community of passionate riders, making every ride an authentic experience that reflects its iconic, rugged image.
- Influential authenticity: An offering that surpasses its essential utility to provoke change. Influential authenticity is when a brand or company stays true to its values and uses that honesty to make a real impact. It's about being genuine and doing the right thing, not just talking about it. This authenticity shapes culture, inspires people, and can even change entire industries by leading purposefully and consistently. Chobani's focus on producing wholesome, natural yogurt and its commitment to social responsibility makes it a standout brand. They've influenced the food industry by promoting transparency in labeling and supporting community programs, including their focus on refugee employment.
- Fake authenticity happens when a brand pretends to be genuine or rooted in values, but it's mostly for show. Disney often leans into this with its "magic" narrative, creating an idealized, fantasy world that doesn't reflect real life. Similarly, Las Vegas markets itself as a place of pure excitement and thrill, but much of its "authentic" charm is built on carefully crafted illusions. Fake can be fun when it's clear that it is

intentionally over the top. The key is that people enjoy it because they know it's not meant to be taken seriously—it's all about the experience and the fun of diving into something imaginary or exaggerated.

CONSIDER authenticity as a back-and-forth between who you are, the world, and what's expected of you. It starts with knowing yourself—figuring out your core values and beliefs—and ensuring your actions match them. That's the heart of genuine authenticity. But it doesn't stop there. Authenticity grows as you interact with others, shaped by cultural norms and your community values. It's about staying true to yourself while understanding and responding to the world you're part of.

Being authentic also means expressing yourself in a way that feels real to you but makes sense to your audience. It's not about seeking approval but ignoring how your actions land with others. Authenticity isn't something you lock in and forget; it changes as you grow and your surroundings evolve. The trick is balancing staying grounded in your identity while adapting to life's shifts without losing your sense of self. At its core, authenticity is about blending your inner truth with your outer connections, creating a dynamic mix of personal honesty and social awareness.

Relevance

Authenticity in marketing is critical because people are drawn to brands that feel real and stay true to their values. Take Coca-Cola, for example. They've built their identity around happiness, togetherness, and refreshment. Campaigns like "Open Happiness" and their focus on connecting people across cultures reflect these core themes. By sticking to this message of positivity and shared experiences, Coca-Cola has created a strong emotional bond with consumers, earning loyalty around the globe.

Walmart takes a different approach to authenticity, focusing on affordability and accessibility for everyone. Its "Save Money. Live Better" slogan isn't just a tagline—it reflects its mission to provide essential products at prices people can trust. Behind the scenes, Walmart follows its "Everyday Low Cost" strategy, passing it on to customers through "Everyday Low Prices." Walmart's ads often feature relatable families and real-life scenarios, reinforcing its image as a brand that genuinely understands its shoppers' needs.

When brands fail to live up to their promises, though, it's obvious. If a company claims to care about sustainability or ethics but doesn't back it up, people notice—and trust disappears fast. Authenticity isn't just a buzzword; it keeps brands like Walmart and Coca-Cola connected to their customers and building long-term loyalty.

AT THE *TRUST* LEVEL, the following psychological motivations are crucial to understand and cater to:

- **Uniqueness:** The most critical umbrella motivation.

- Real
- Sanctuary

- Choice
- Comfort
- Pride

RELATED MARKETING CONCEPTS ARE:

- Care
- Genuine
- Honesty
- Faithful
- Retro

CASE EXAMPLE
Southwest

BACKGROUND

Southwest Airlines started in 1967 with a big idea and a simple plan. Herb Kelleher and Rollin King wanted to make air travel affordable and accessible, focusing on quick, low-cost flights between Dallas, Houston, and San Antonio. To avoid high costs tied to federal regulations, they operated exclusively within Texas, sketching their "Texas Triangle" route map on a napkin. Their mission was clear: democratize air travel and bring it to the masses.

When Southwest launched flights in 1971, the road wasn't smooth. Established airlines fought them with lawsuits, and financial struggles loomed early on. But

Southwest had innovative tricks up its sleeve. They turned planes around faster than competitors, keeping them in the air and cutting costs. By using secondary airports like Houston Hobby, they avoided expensive hubs, which helped them stay competitive. By 1973, they had turned their first profit, setting the stage for growth.

Southwest expanded carefully, moving from Texas routes to a national network while sticking to its roots: low fares and friendly service. Its "no-frills" model ditched extras like in-flight meals and focused on simplicity. Southwest operated only Boeing 737s to streamline maintenance and training. It introduced open seating and quirky, humorous onboard announcements, making flights efficient and fun. This unique personality resonated with passengers and set Southwest apart.

As they grew, Southwest proved it wasn't just about cutting costs—they prioritized their employees and customers. Their strong corporate culture, built on respect, satisfaction, and a little humor, became a cornerstone of their success. Even during challenging times in the airline industry, Southwest stayed profitable and resilient, earning a reputation as one of the best-managed airlines.

Today, Southwest is a major player in U.S. air travel and a global inspiration for low-cost carriers like Ryanair and EasyJet in Europe. By adhering to its core values of simplicity, affordability, and service, Southwest has built a legacy that has lasted more than five decades and continues to thrive.

Performance

Southwest Airlines has seen remarkable growth in size and financial performance over the years, proving that its low-cost business model is more than just a strategy—it's a cornerstone of its success. The airline has built a strong customer base and solid financial foundation, enabling it to tackle industry challenges while achieving impressive revenue growth. After the brutal hit in 2020, Southwest bounced back with a vengeance, boosting its annual revenue from $15.79 billion in 2021 to $26.09 billion in 2023. By 2024, its revenue climbed even higher, reaching $27.38 billion—a 7.61% jump year-over-year that shows how resilient the airline has become.

ONE OF SOUTHWEST'S secret weapons is its savvy use of fuel hedging. By locking in fuel prices in advance, they protect themselves from sudden price hikes, keeping costs steady and fares competitive. In 2023, this strategy stabilized expenses and improved fuel efficiency by 4%, aligning with the airline's reputation for intelligent, efficient operations. The airline's fleet upgrades to the Boeing 737-8, a more fuel-efficient aircraft, further underscore its commitment to cost savings and sustainability.

SOUTHWEST'S GROWTH isn't just about numbers; it's about staying ahead in a challenging market. By adding new routes and focusing on operational efficiency, they expand their reach without losing the affordability and reliability that customers love. This balance of intelligent financial management and customer service keeps Southwest thriving in an industry where many others struggle to stay afloat.

BECOMING ESSENTIAL FACTOR: Transparent authenticity

. . .

Southwest Airlines is an authentic passenger choice thanks to its no-nonsense, customer-first approach. People trust Southwest because it keeps things simple and transparent. Southwest will introduce assigned seating starting in late 2025, replacing its traditional open seating policy. Seat selection will depend on the fare type: higher fare categories include free assignments, while the lowest fare, "Wanna Get Away," excludes complimentary selection but allows paid upgrades. Premium seating, such as extra-legroom options, will also be available for an additional fee. This shift reflects customer feedback and aims to offer more flexibility and choices.

What sets Southwest apart is its culture, which starts with its employees. The airline's team is known for being friendly and down-to-earth, often adding a personal touch to the flying experience. Flight attendants don't just stick to scripts; they'll crack jokes, share a laugh, or brighten the mood with playful announcements. This relaxed, genuine energy makes flying Southwest feel less like a chore and more like a casual, enjoyable journey, which passengers appreciate in a sometimes stressful industry.

Southwest backs up its talk of putting "Customers first" with actions. It prioritizes on-time performance and handles inevitable delays with transparency, keeping passengers informed and in the loop. This proactive communication builds trust, showing that the airline genuinely cares about its customers' time and experience. From booking to landing, Southwest focuses on making things as smooth as possible, earning loyalty by consistently living up to its promises. This mix of affordability, honesty, and a human touch makes the brand feel real to so many people.

LEARNINGS

HOW TO MAKE it work in your offering:

- Key Customer Driver: Uniqueness
    - The one-of-a-kind factor benefits the brand and its users since users receive an experience no other brand can provide. The one-of-a-kind factor creates a win-win situation for the brand and its users. For the brand, it establishes a unique identity that sets it apart from competitors, making it memorable and desirable in a crowded marketplace. This uniqueness often becomes a key selling point, driving loyalty and encouraging word-of-mouth recommendations. The benefit is even more personal for users—they gain access to an experience, product, or service they can't get anywhere else. It's not just about functionality or utility but the emotional value of engaging with something distinctive. Whether it's an innovative feature, a personalized experience, or a bold new approach, the one-of-a-kind factor leaves a

lasting impression and deepens the bond between the user and the brand.

- What to Identify: A brand behavior that meets people's expectations.
    - Authentic brand behavior is about a brand genuinely standing by what it believes in and consistently showing it in everything it does. It's not about putting on a show or chasing trends; it's about being real and honest so people can trust that what they see is what they get. For example, a company that promotes fair trade doesn't just slap a label on its products—it actively ensures workers are paid fairly and treated well. Similarly, a tech brand focused on innovation backs that up by constantly improving its products, not just hyping them up. When a brand truly lives out its values in every aspect—whether in customer interactions, how it operates, or even how it handles challenges—it creates a deeper connection with people. That's the kind of authenticity customers notice and respect.

- "Essential" Insert: Genuine components—an honest voice.
    - A great example of emphasizing authenticity is Whole Foods, known for offering organic

and high-quality food options; it consistently meets the expectations of health-conscious consumers. By focusing on quality products, sustainability, and transparency, the brand ensures customers can trust that what they're buying aligns with their values around healthy eating and environmental responsibility. Shoppers go to Whole Foods because they know they'll find fresh, nutritious food options that align with their lifestyle. The brand is also transparent about where its food comes from, which is essential for many customers who care about ethical and environmental issues. Another critical way Whole Foods meets expectations is its commitment to sustainability, from eco-friendly packaging to sourcing products that meet high environmental and ethical standards. Whole Foods' commitment to sustainability is rooted in honesty.

- Key Customer Reward: Pride halo
    - A brand's authenticity emphasis can become a "badge of honor." When people feel they are supporting a brand that is genuine, transparent, and aligned with their values, it often boosts their pride. They see themselves as part of something real—whether it's supporting sustainability, ethical business practices, or simply a company that values honesty over flashy marketing tactics. This

badge of honor can also extend to how consumers view their identity. When they choose brands that emphasize authenticity, they often feel that their purchasing decisions reflect their values. It's almost like aligning themselves with a brand that "gets it" and that shares their perspective.

- Brand Becomes: Street real
    - For a brand to become "street real," it must connect with people naturally and unpretentiously. It avoids pretensions, making its authenticity visible through its actions, products, and culture. This approach makes the brand feel less corporate and more like something that truly belongs in everyday life. Customers then see it as not just another company but a brand that speaks their language and fits into their real-world experiences. It becomes relatable, trusted, and earned—not just sold but shared.

IN SUMMARY:

YOU WILL UPGRADE your offering from "trustable" to "true."

11

ESSENTIAL RECOMMENDATIONS

 word of advice

BEFORE DISCUSSING some crucial aspects of working with the different Becoming Essential ways, it's important to reflect on how these varied strategies came to be and how they should be applied.

They all start with a proven model or theory that supports their validity and, most importantly, their effectiveness. Many real-life business examples support that claim. At the same time, each chapter details the underpinnings, showing the foundational elements that facilitate its application to any business size and category.

The ten ways do not function as plug-and-play solutions; they require careful observation of two key factors:

- Landscape: This represents the broader environment in which your business operates. It includes analyzing industry trends, competitive dynamics, and evolving customer preferences. It's about understanding the unique challenges and opportunities within your market. Are shifting technologies, economic conditions, or regulatory changes impacting the market?

The landscape also requires you to identify gaps where your business can innovate or stand out by analyzing areas that competitors might overlook or addressing unsatisfied market needs. These gaps could manifest as unmet customer expectations, inefficiencies in existing solutions, or opportunities arising from emerging technologies or trends.

For instance, consider whether customers face specific pain points that current offerings fail to address. Reflect on whether your business can simplify a complex process or deliver more excellent value at a lower cost. Explore whether your market has underserved niches that larger competitors ignore or cannot effectively serve.

By identifying and targeting these gaps, you can position your business to offer something unique through product innovation, superior customer service, or a fresh marketing approach. This thoroughness differentiates your brand and builds resilience against the competition by anchoring your strategy in opportunities tailored to your market's needs.

- Ecosystem: This book examines an ecosystem through the lens of internal marketing teams resisting change. The ecosystem becomes more than a network of resources and relationships; it transforms into a cultural and psychological environment that shapes strategies. Teams often resist change because they feel comfortable with current processes, fear the unknown, or doubt the value of new approaches.

To overcome this resistance, you must nurture the internal ecosystem and create an environment where change feels natural and exciting. Start by fostering open communication. Clearly explain the "why" behind new strategies and connect them directly to team goals and success stories. When marketing teams feel included in decision-making, they take ownership of changes, which reduces the feeling of having strategies imposed on them.

The ecosystem should also encourage learning and experimentation. Resistance softens when teams have the tools and training to adapt and the freedom to test new ideas without fearing failure. Leaders play a crucial role by modeling adaptability, celebrating small wins, and showing how new strategies deliver real results.

By viewing the ecosystem this way, you can focus on human dynamics. Building trust, easing friction, and aligning incentives within the team environment turn resistance into collaboration, ensuring changes are accepted and successfully implemented.

Analyzing the different dynamics before moving any pieces will pay off in the long run. The best time to consider all the possibilities is at the beginning. Once you make a move, it's clear that it will start costing money and resources, draining your finances and eroding your credibility and mental energy as you continue to push forward.

The following is a deep dive into your considerations before applying any of the ten Becoming Essential ways. While they are discrete, their combined use is still possible. Remember that this book is about whetting your appetite for a better and original way of conducting your business.

ESSENTIAL CHECKLIST

#1: Are your competitors using any of the "10 BE Ways?"

BEFORE EMBARKING on any path toward becoming essential, you'll need to determine which Ways are already in use within the incumbent category. Your goal here is to construct a "category construct," typically represented as a mapping with four distinct quadrants or, in more dynamic marketing environments, an evolving continuum. Mapping allows you to visualize and understand the landscape of available options.

Each quadrant represents a distinct approach or positioning, helping to highlight where competitors are focusing their efforts. For example, one quadrant might show brands emphasizing innovation, another might highlight those focused on price leadership, and a third could center on premium quality or customer experience.

However, in rapidly evolving markets or industries with frequent shifts in customer preferences, a category construct can also take the form of a continuum. This construct allows for a more fluid view, reflecting how brands or offerings evolve. The continuum acknowledges that the competitive landscape is dynamic, and brands may shift their positioning as customer expectations change or new technologies emerge.

Creating a category construct involves gathering data on how current competitors position themselves and identifying the critical factors that customers care about. It might also include mapping consumer perceptions and behaviors to ensure the construct aligns with how the market views the category. This exercise is crucial for understanding where gaps or opportunities exist, enabling brands to identify untapped areas for growth or innovation.

Your chosen "BE Way" must withstand a comparison test of relevancy and appeal against what your competitors offer. This exercise isn't just about differentiation—it's about building something that resonates deeply and maintains its attractiveness over time, standing out not just in terms of what it offers but how it connects with your audience.

#2: Is your target already overexposed to your chosen "BE Way"?

COVERING your competitors won't cut it if you aren't paying attention to whether players from other categories are reaching your target audience with their own "BE Ways." Today's market is incredibly interconnected, and the lines between categories are often blurred. Brands in different sectors may be competing for the same attention from your target demographic and psychographics without you even realizing it. It's not enough to only worry about what your direct competitors are doing—you also have to look at the bigger picture. To fully understand where you stand, you need to dive deeper into other categories that are also trying to capture your audience's interest.

THINK ABOUT IT—OTHER categories, even if they don't seem directly related to your product, could attract your audience by offering something that overlaps with your "BE Way." So, you must analyze which categories view your target market as their primary focus. How are they reaching that same audience? What strategies are they using? It's about identifying the more prominent players who are going after the same consumers and recognizing where there might be similarities or crossover in how they engage them. Look at the media strategy they're using, their messages, and how they're positioning themselves to draw your audience in.

THIS ANALYSIS DOESN'T JUST HELP you identify your competitors more broadly but opens your eyes to potential threats you hadn't considered. For example, a brand in a completely different industry might be addressing the same need you're targeting or offering a similar benefit in a way that appeals to your audience. The key is spotting where those overlaps exist so you can adjust your strategy accordingly and avoid being blindsided by indirect competition.

ONCE YOU'VE MAPPED out these overlaps, your selected "BE Way" has to pass the comparison test of uniqueness. Being different is not enough—it's about being distinct and meaningful. Your "BE Way" needs to offer something that's not just new to the market but something that provides a unique value to your audience. You have to ensure that what you're offering stands out, not only against your direct competitors but also against what consumers already receive from other categories. If they're getting a similar experience, message, or value from brands outside your category, it will be hard for you to grab their attention and loyalty.

It is critical to understand what your audience is already experiencing from those other categories and ensure your "BE Way" offers fresh and necessary things. This understanding isn't just about filling a gap—it's about providing a differentiated experience that makes your audience feel like they're gaining something valuable by choosing your brand. Your approach must resonate with them in a personal and irreplaceable way. If you don't do this, even if your competitors cover their bases, you may fail to become essential to your audience.

One classic tool for analyzing competitors and realizing your brand's possibilities is SWOT analysis. A SWOT analysis is a strategic planning tool for assessing Strengths, Weaknesses, Opportunities, and Threats related to a business, project, or product. It helps identify internal and external factors that impact success and guides decision-making and planning.

Strengths are internal factors that give a business an advantage over competitors. They can include a strong brand, unique product features, a skilled workforce, financial stability, or technological advantages. Strengths are what your business does well or the resources it has that help it achieve goals.

WEAKNESSES ARE internal factors that create disadvantages. These include outdated technology, poor brand recognition, financial constraints, or operational inefficiencies. Identifying weaknesses helps businesses develop strategies to address or mitigate them.

OPPORTUNITIES ARE external factors that represent favorable conditions for growth or gaining a competitive edge. These might be emerging market trends, new technologies, changes in consumer behavior, or favorable regulations. Recognizing opportunities allows businesses to capitalize on these conditions proactively.

THREATS ARE external factors that could harm the business. These can come from competitors, market changes, economic shifts, technological disruptions, or new regulations. Identifying threats helps businesses prepare for challenges and adjust strategies to reduce negative impacts.

TO USE SWOT EFFECTIVELY, you analyze both internal and external elements. Strengths and weaknesses are within your control and can be adjusted, while external opportunities and threats require adaptation.

For example, a business might have a loyal customer base (strength) but face high production costs (weakness).

Growing demand for eco-friendly products could be an opportunity, while new competitors offering lower prices could be a threat.

A SWOT ANALYSIS provides insights into a business's position, helping leverage strengths, address weaknesses, capitalize on opportunities, and prepare for threats. This tool can be used periodically to track changes or make decisions like product launches or market expansions.

#3: Make a side-by-side comparison between your chosen "BE Way" and your consumer's Needstates.

TAKE a step back and examine your product or service through the lens of what truly drives consumer behavior: their three core need states. These aren't abstract or fleeting concepts—they're the fundamental rhythms of daily life. Every day, every person cycles through these needs, often unconsciously. Understanding them gives you a decisive edge. Let's unpack each one:

1. Heal: This is all about restoring balance and protecting well-being. Think of those moments when people are physically, mentally, or emotionally drained. They're seeking relief, recovery, and defense against further strain. Whether it's a soothing tea, a skincare product, or even a calming app, offerings that help people heal become essential parts of their habits.

. . .

2. Balance: Here, people are looking for stability and reinforcement. It's about ensuring they can handle their day smoothly. This needstate might mean a midday snack to keep energy steady, a productivity tool that streamlines their tasks, or even an inspirational podcast that lifts their spirits. Products in this space must quietly but reliably support the consumer's journey.

3. Boost: This is the surge of energy, the recharge people crave to keep moving forward or tackle challenges. Boost moments call for products or services that invigorate, inspire, and prepare people to take on the next big thing. From energizing beverages to workout gear or motivational content, your offering should leave them feeling entirely driven.

YOU'VE LIKELY HEARD the saying, *"Don't go grocery shopping on an empty stomach."* It's a perfect example of how closely our needs and moods are intertwined. When people feel depleted, their decisions reflect that. Similarly, when consumers encounter your offering, they subconsciously ask, *"Does this meet my needs—right now, and better than anything else I already have?"*

. . .

Now, here's where your opportunity lies. Review your "BE" strategy by focusing on how your product aligns with one or more of these core need states. The key isn't just addressing a need but doing so in a distinct, meaningful, and indispensable way.

ASK YOURSELF:

- How does my offering help people heal, balance, or boost their day?
- Does it stand out from the competition?
- Is it intuitive and easy for them to see its value?

THIS EXERCISE ISN'T JUST about creating something useful—it's about embedding your offering into the consumer's life so seamlessly that they rely on it without hesitation. Your "BE Way" must become an integral solution that doesn't just compete but outshines. When you design your product with these need states at its core, you're no longer selling an item—you're delivering an experience that resonates deeply and repeatedly. Take this insight and refine your approach. The consumer isn't just buying your product or service but investing in how it fits into their life and fulfills their daily shifting needs.

#4: Make sure your selected "BE Way" is in harmony with your Brand Pyramid

. . .

To complete your analysis, you must check it against what your brand stands for and can sustain over time. The Brand Pyramid provides all the necessary checkpoints to evaluate whether your chosen "BE Way" enhances or conflicts with your brand, particularly at the attributes, benefits, and essence levels. Your selected "BE Way" must pass the test of improving your current proposal as outlined in the Brand Pyramid.

The brand pyramid is a valuable model for understanding how a brand grows and becomes more than a product or service. It's a hierarchy of how a brand connects with people, starting with the most basic functions and moving to more meaningful, emotional connections.

At the base of the pyramid, you've got the functional benefits, where the brand delivers practical, tangible benefits like solving a problem, being reliable, or offering convenience. At this level, customers start paying attention to a brand because it meets their basic needs. For example, a car brand might offer fuel efficiency or safety, or a tech company might provide ease of use. These benefits are the foundation of what customers initially value about the product.

Next comes the emotional benefits level. As a brand grows, it starts to connect with people beyond just the practical benefits. At this point, customers feel something when they interact with the brand. It could be a sense of excitement, trust, or nostalgia. For instance, Apple doesn't just sell tech products—it sells a feeling of being part of a creative, forward-thinking community. This emotional connection often drives brand loyalty and helps people form a more profound attachment to the brand.

ABOVE THAT, you reach the brand values level, where the brand communicates what it stands for beyond its products. Brands with solid values align with causes or principles that resonate with their audience. Take Patagonia, for example. Its commitment to environmental sustainability goes beyond selling outdoor gear—it actively promotes ecological activism. When a brand's values resonate with customers' beliefs or aspirations, it forms a deeper bond that transcends the functional and emotional benefits.

THEN, as you move higher, you encounter brand personality. This level is about the tone, voice, and character that the brand expresses. A brand's personality shapes how it interacts with customers and how people perceive it in everyday life. Think of Nike with its bold, empowering voice, or Coca-Cola, which has a friendly and inclusive personality. A strong personality gives the brand a unique identity, making it more relatable and human. It helps customers feel like they "know" the brand and trust it more.

AT THE TOP of the pyramid, you've got brand essence, the heart of the brand—the core truth that defines everything the brand is about. It's the unspoken promise or feeling that the brand conveys in everything it does. It's usually abstract, like Nike's "Just Do It," which encapsulates empowerment, perseverance, and motivation. The brand essence ties all the lower levels together, providing consistency and clarity. It makes the brand unforgettable and sticks in people's minds long after interacting with it.

IN ESSENCE, the brand pyramid shows how a brand can move from offering a simple product or service to becoming a significant part of someone's life. It's not just about what the brand provides but about how it makes people feel and what it represents. The higher a brand climbs on the pyramid, the more it becomes a part of people's identities and daily lives. This process helps brands build loyalty, create a lasting impact, and even turn customers into advocates who feel personally invested in the brand's success.

#5: PROTECT YOUR "BE" enhanced offering by pre-empting moves from your competitors

ONCE YOU CHOOSE and start using a specific "BE Way," you might face new challenges when competitors respond to your updated approach. They won't just sit back—they'll react, and their moves could put your strategy to the test. To stay ahead, you'll need to think a few steps ahead. Predicting how your key competitors might respond becomes essential. It's not enough to react now; you must prepare your Brand's counter-moves in advance.

THE STRATEGY you've chosen has to hold up against the pressure of a competitive market where everyone is looking for an edge. It's like a game of chess, where every move you make invites a counter from your opponent. Your "BE Way" needs to prove it's more than just a great idea—it has to show strength and resilience. It must handle the heat of direct competition and still come out ahead. And it's not just about winning once; your strategy has to stay sharp and relevant over time, consistently maintaining its advantage while adapting to the ever-changing playing field.

CHESS-LIKE MARKETING TOOLS and frameworks help brands anticipate moves and counter-moves in competitive environments. These tools focus on strategy, foresight, and positioning to stay ahead of the competition. The following are two essential tools:

1. Decision trees: Decision trees are a simple yet powerful way to make strategic decisions by breaking them into smaller, manageable steps. Picture a tree where each branch represents a possible choice, and every subsequent branch shows what could happen next based on that choice. It's like plotting out your options in a game, step by step, to see the possible outcomes.

HERE'S HOW IT WORKS: You start with a decision point—your brand decides whether to launch a new product. The first branches would be "Yes" and "No." From there, each branch splits into what could happen next. If you launch, you may predict strong sales but risk a competitor copying you. If you don't launch, you might save money but miss a significant market opportunity. By continuing to break these down—maybe factoring in costs, potential customer responses, and competitor actions—you can follow each path and weigh the risks and rewards.

EXAMPLE: Imagine you own a neighborhood restaurant and are deciding whether to offer delivery. People love dining in, but delivery demand is growing, and competitors are already in the game. A decision tree helps you think ahead, especially when considering how competitors will react.

IF YOU LAUNCH DELIVERY, you might attract new customers and boost sales. But competitors won't sit back. They'll likely mimic your service, undercut prices, or run aggressive promotions. They might even enhance delivery, adding faster times or exclusive deals to outshine you. Without preparation, your early success could falter in a price war or logistics battle.

IF YOU SKIP A DELIVERY, loyal customers might still fill your tables. But competitors could pounce on your absence, positioning themselves as the go-to option for convenience and targeting your customer base directly. Over time, you risk losing relevance as they dominate the delivery space.

A DECISION TREE not only maps your choices but anticipates competitor moves. For example, if you launch delivery, you might add rewards programs or focus on unique offerings competitors can't copy. By thinking strategically, you stay a step ahead, treating this as more than just a decision—it's a chess match where planning their counter is as vital as your move.

2. AI: Artificial intelligence (AI) takes predictive analytics to the next level by learning and adapting in real-time. AI doesn't just analyze past data; it uses machine learning to get smarter as it processes new information. It can spot patterns you might miss, adjust predictions as conditions change, and even automate decisions based on what it learns.

HERE'S HOW IT WORKS: AI algorithms sift through vast amounts of data—everything from customer reviews to competitor pricing—and identify trends. Then, they use that information to recommend or even execute actions. For example, an AI system might notice that customers in one region are more likely to buy certain products and automatically adjust your ad targeting to focus on that area.

EXAMPLE: Think about Netflix. Their AI tracks what you watch, how long you watch it, and even when you pause or rewind. Using this data, it predicts what you're likely to enjoy next and recommends it to you. For marketers, this same kind of AI could personalize email campaigns, suggest products, or even tweak pricing to match what customers are most likely to respond to.

. . .

#6: Plan for your chosen "BE Way" to fit future opportunities brought by industry trends and shifts in the culture

Your chosen "BE Way" acts as a compass, guiding the brand through the inevitable shifts in its category, consumer expectations, and even its essence as it evolves or crosses into new territories. Markets are alive—they grow, contract, and transform in response to societal changes, technological advances, and shifting consumer priorities. To stay ahead of the curve and competitors, your offering must remain relevant and adapt while staying true to its core promise. This state of alertness means your "BE Way" should be dynamic and resilient, designed to hold its value even as the world changes.

Scenario planning becomes crucial in this process, allowing you to prepare for the unexpected and design a roadmap for different possible futures. For instance, let's say your category begins to tilt heavily toward sustainability, driven by new regulations or a dramatic shift in consumer priorities toward eco-friendly products. Using scenario planning, you could explore this possibility in depth: What would your market look like in five years if this trend takes over? How might competitors react? What changes would your brand need to make to align with this movement without losing its essence?

. . .

EVEN IF YOUR business lacks the sophistication of larger companies, scenario planning can still be effective without being overly complicated. By staying proactive, thinking creatively, and preparing for different possible futures in a structured yet simple way, you can make this tool work for your needs. The key is using straightforward techniques that are practical and easy to implement.

START by identifying the core uncertainties your business faces. These could be external factors like changing consumer trends, new regulations, or economic shifts. For example, will customers in your category demand more digital experiences, or will there be a resurgence of in-person engagement? Once you identify these uncertainties, focus on those most likely to impact your business.

NEXT, create a few simple, plausible scenarios. Aim for 3-4 distinct possibilities rather than overloading with endless variations. For instance, if you're in retail, you might map out one future where e-commerce dominates, another where physical stores remain crucial, a hybrid scenario blending both, and a curveball scenario where global supply chain disruptions reshape the landscape entirely. Keep these scenarios clear and relatable—your goal is to spark practical conversations, not overwhelm with detail.

FROM THERE, brainstorm how your business would respond in each situation. Ask questions like, "How would we stay competitive?" or "What would our customers need from us in this future?" Keep the discussion open, involving key team members to ensure diverse perspectives. This step isn't about perfecting everything but identifying a few strategic moves that could work across multiple scenarios.

FINALLY, use the insights from your scenarios to stress-test your current strategy. Does your brand's "BE Way" hold up in all your envisioned futures? For example, if sustainability becomes non-negotiable, is your offering ready? If digital engagement takes center stage, are you equipped to deliver? The idea is to uncover gaps and opportunities so your strategy becomes more resilient.

FOR A MEDIUM-SIZED BUSINESS, this doesn't require fancy software or consultants. A few team meetings, whiteboard sessions, and focused discussions are often enough to get started. The most important outcome is not predicting the future but ensuring your business can adapt and thrive no matter the market's direction. Scenario planning is less about complexity and more about clarity, helping you build confidence in your ability to navigate whatever comes next.

#7: WANT TO COMBINE "BE WAYS"? **Make it a two-step evolution**

WHEN TACKLING a challenge with a two-step evolution, approach it as a deliberate and strategic journey. This process isn't about rushing to solutions but building a solid foundation for lasting impact. The first step begins with selecting a "BE Way" that injects new life into the brand.

Maybe it's about reimagining the brand's core message or infusing it with fresh energy to capture attention and inspire excitement.

This step acts as the catalyst, sparking momentum and creating the conditions needed for meaningful transformation. With the initial spark ignited, the second step solidifies the brand's direction. Here, you'll choose a "BE Way" that isn't just relevant for today but is built to stand the test of time. This phase defines the brand's enduring identity, ensuring it resonates with its audience and adapts to future challenges. The two steps work hand in hand—one creating the spark, the other establishing the anchor.

It's essential to evaluate how these steps align and interact. They must complement each other, creating a seamless flow that supports the overall brand strategy. A mismatch between the two could create confusion or dilute the brand's message. Instead, aim for harmony—a straightforward, cohesive narrative that strengthens the brand's position and leaves a lasting impression. Through this thoughtful and layered approach, your brand evolves with intention and resilience, ensuring it remains relevant, compelling, and accurate to its core purpose.

Connectivity to Ritualization examples:

Here are examples of brands that successfully moved from connectivity to ritualization:

. . .

1. Starbucks

    - Connectivity: Starbucks initially focused on creating a "third place" between home and work where people could connect, relax, or collaborate. This idea of connectivity was central to their success, making Starbucks a go-to spot for communities, friends, and professionals.
    - Ritualization: Over time, Starbucks became ritualized in people's daily lives. Morning coffee stops, specific drink orders, and the experience of personalized service turned visiting Starbucks into a habit. Introducing loyalty programs like Starbucks Rewards further embedded Starbucks into routines, enhancing the sense of ritual.

2. Peloton

    - Connectivity: Peloton began by building a community of fitness enthusiasts who connected virtually through live and on-demand workouts. The ability to interact with instructors and other users in real-time made fitness feel communal and engaging, even at home.
    - Ritualization: Peloton evolved into a ritual by making its platform part of users' daily routines. Regular classes, leaderboards, and personalized progress tracking turned Peloton from a fitness

tool into a lifestyle. It's not just a workout—an expected, repeated activity that defines their day.

Authenticity to Making It Easy Examples

1. Amazon

- Authenticity: Amazon began authentically as an online bookstore with a mission to provide a vast selection and competitive pricing. Their authenticity lies in their relentless focus on customer satisfaction.
- Making It Easy: Amazon became synonymous with ease by introducing innovations like one-click ordering, Prime two-day shipping, and a comprehensive ecosystem of services like Alexa and Amazon Fresh. They simplified the shopping experience while maintaining their commitment to being "Earth's most customer-centric company."

2. Tesla

- Authenticity: Tesla's authenticity stemmed from its mission to accelerate the transition to sustainable energy through innovative, eco-conscious electric vehicles.

- Making It Easy: Tesla focused on ease by designing cars with over-the-air software updates, a seamless online purchasing experience, and features like the Tesla Supercharger network. They made owning an electric vehicle not just desirable but incredibly convenient.

#8: Not all "BE Ways" are helpful for all challenges. Shortlist them to get to the ones with more potential

When you explore the ten "BE Ways," you might notice that some don't feel quite right for your current needs or even seem to fit your category. That's fine because these approaches span many industries, not just yours. Think of them as tools in a versatile toolkit—some will be perfect for the job, while others won't be necessary right now. The key is to narrow down your options to a focused shortlist. Start by setting aside the ideas that don't show much promise, are already overused in your category, or feel like they would overwhelm your audience because they're so common in other areas.

Take a snack brand, for instance. If most competitors focus on health benefits, you might not follow the crowd. Instead, you could focus on something different, like "fun and shareability," emphasizing the joy of eating with friends. Pringles does this well with its playful stackable design, which encourages creativity and interaction. Or, let's say you're entering the personal care space. If eco-friendly messaging dominates, you might stand out by highlighting simplicity and reliability, much like how Dove focuses on authenticity and straightforward care.

Your shortlist should reflect ideas that align with your brand's strengths and goals. Each "BE Way" you choose must show potential to boost your brand equity and sales. For instance, if you're in fashion, you might skip the saturated high-end luxury angle and embrace inclusivity. A brand that celebrates all body types or offers affordable, stylish options for everyone can carve out a meaningful and lasting niche.

The final choices should go beyond what looks good on paper. They must resonate with your audience, spark interest, and provide clear benefits. When executed well, these approaches will give your brand the staying power it needs to grow while helping you avoid getting lost in competitors' noise.

The following guides help you with your ideation sessions while dealing with your situation. Remember that every brand situation presents different opportunities in terms of market, target, categories, and overall surrounding conditions.

Step 1: Identify the best examples and extract key learnings from them:

- List the ten "BE Ways."
- List the "BE Ways" brand examples in your market and what you are learning from that information.
- List the "BE Ways" brand examples in your category and what you are learning from that information.
- List the "BE Ways" customer target examples in your market and what you are learning from that information.

STEP 2: Select your best opportunities from the ten "BE Ways," then refine your current offering with the following four fields:

- Motivation/s to add to your offering.
- Barrier/s to remove from your offering.
- Features to increase your offering.
- Features to reduce from your offering.

#9: Avoid settling for the obvious "BE Ways." Consider each one and give it a fair chance.

As you go through the "10 BE Ways," some will naturally stand out more than others. They might seem like safer choices, but it's worth taking the time to consider all ten before ruling any out. Options like "Talk Survival" or "Become a Routine" might grab your attention immediately

—they're familiar and could deliver quick wins. However, looking closely at the others could reveal less obvious opportunities but potentially more impactful in the long run.

TAKE A LOCAL GYM, for example. It could easily focus on "Become a Routine," encouraging people to show up daily and build habits. However, exploring "Facilitate Connectivity" could create a stronger emotional bond by hosting events or challenges that foster connections among members. Or think of a bakery that, instead of offering a wide variety of breads and sweets, focuses on "Embrace Cultural Needs," offering cultural and ethnic specialties or the value of providing quality artisan products.

YOUR SHORTLIST SHOULD REFLECT A THOUGHTFUL, well-rounded evaluation of each option. It's not just about going for what's easy or obvious—it's about finding the "BE Ways" that align with your brand's strengths and create lasting impact. Approaching it this way ensures your choices have depth and meaning, helping your brand build equity while staying true to its core identity.

#10: Make your offering stronger

SOME OF THE TEN "BE WAYS" might seem appealing at first glance, especially because specific options, like the harmonization suggested by "Deal With the 3 Brains," come across as more accessible or more comfortable to tackle. It's natural to gravitate toward what feels manageable or familiar, but this is where many people go wrong. Choosing comfort over substance distorts how these approaches function. "Deal With the 3 Brains" doesn't aim to simplify things for you. Instead, it unlocks the power of harmonizing all your customer's needs and wants.

When used as intended, it's a powerful tool. When misused or approached with the wrong mindset, it loses effectiveness and becomes another checkbox on a to-do list. The right way to approach this isn't to ask, *"What feels good to me?"* but rather, "What has the potential to create a real, lasting impact on the brand?" or *"What makes this offering stand out in a way that's unique?"* These aren't easy questions, but they're essential. Starting with comfort as your guiding principle limits what you can achieve. You produce shallow revisions, and the final result mirrors that lack of depth—ordinary, forgettable, and ultimately unremarkable.

To make the most of these "BE Ways," you must ensure that your choice can withstand the test of relevance and salience. This process isn't just about tweaking your offering; it's about creating something bold enough to be noticed, fresh sufficient to spark interest, and distinctive enough to redefine how your audience perceives your brand. When your revised offering hits the market, it should feel like something entirely new, not just a slight upgrade of what already exists.

. . .

Salience is key. With it, your work will be able to break through the noise of the marketplace. The ten "BE Ways" are not shortcuts to comfort; they're frameworks for transformation. They demand focus, effort, and a willingness to step into what's challenging. When done correctly, they ensure that what you create is not just another version of the same old thing but something that commands attention, sparks excitement, and delivers lasting value.

12

ESSENTIAL BOOKS

Talk Survival

BOOK 1: The Theory

Paul W. King's "Climbing Maslow's Pyramid" walks you through Maslow's Hierarchy of Needs, showing how to move from survival to self-discovery and fulfillment. It breaks down the steps in relatable, actionable ways, helping you master the essentials while unlocking your potential at every level. Practical insights and a fresh perspective reveal how meeting foundational needs creates the launchpad for growth, purpose, and thriving in life.

BOOK 2: Marketing Application

Chip Conley's "Peak: How Great Companies Get Their Mojo from Maslow" reimagines Abraham Maslow's Hierarchy of Needs as a framework for business and leadership.

Conley explains how companies can thrive by addressing the deeper needs of their employees, customers, and investors. Drawing from his experience in the hospitality industry, he demonstrates that fulfilling basic expectations is only the starting point. True success comes from creating emotional connections and delivering transformational experiences that resonate on a higher, more meaningful level. Conley argues that leaders who cultivate purpose and foster a sense of belonging and fulfillment inspire loyalty and achieve sustainable growth. By aligning business practices with human aspirations, "Peak" provides a roadmap for building organizations that thrive on connection and purpose.

ACHIEVE RITUALIZATION

BOOK 1: The Theory
Catherine Bell's "Ritual Theory, Ritual Practice" focuses on how rituals function in society. In ritual theory, she argues that rituals aren't just symbolic acts—they shape and reinforce social order and identity. Bell believes rituals are dynamic, not static, and can change over time depending on cultural, social, and political contexts. Instead of seeing rituals as fixed traditions, she highlights their performative nature and how they reflect power and human agency. Bell looks at how rituals are carried out and experienced daily in ritual practice. She emphasizes that rituals aren't just about following a set script; they involve participation and can be adapted or improvised. Ritual practice is about how people engage with and interpret rituals, making them personal and fluid rather than rigid. For

Bell, rituals are shaped by tradition and the people who perform them.

Book 2: Marketing Application

Chip and Dan Heath's "The Power of Moments" explores how certain moments in experiences can be transformed into unforgettable rituals. While not exclusively about marketing, it offers deep insights into how brands can create experiences that resonate and stick with customers, much like rituals do. The Heath brothers argue that by focusing on the peak moments of an experience, brands can create lasting emotional connections beyond a simple transaction.

Stay Close

Book 1: The Theory

Lisa Fortini-Campbell's "Hitting the Sweet Spot" is a practical workbook focused on leveraging consumer insights to craft effective marketing and advertising strategies. It guides readers through identifying the "sweet spot"—the intersection of what consumers desire and what a brand can uniquely deliver. The book emphasizes understanding consumer behavior and motivation to create compelling campaigns. Actionable exercises and examples aim to help marketers connect emotionally with their audience and develop strategies that resonate, ensuring alignment between consumer needs and business goals.

. . .

BOOK 2: Marketing Application

Arun Sinha's "How to Maximize Marketing for Business" offers strategies for aligning business elements for innovation, competitive advantage, and growth. It emphasizes finding the "sweet spot" in marketing through customer-centric approaches, brand-building, and leadership engagement. Sinha draws on his expertise in senior marketing roles to provide actionable insights for businesses seeking long-term success.

DEAL with the Three Brains

BOOK 1: The Theory

Paul D. MacLean's "The Triune Brain in Evolution" provides an in-depth examination of the brain's evolutionary development into three key components: the reptilian brain (instincts and survival), the limbic brain (emotions and social bonding), and the neocortex (higher-order thinking and reasoning). MacLean explores how these layers interact to influence human behavior, emotional responses, and cognitive functions. The book highlights the practical implications of this model in understanding mental health, behavioral disorders, and the interplay between instinct, emotion, and intellect.

BOOK 2: Marketing Application

Patrick Renvoise and Christophe Morin's "Neuromarketing: Understanding the Buy Buttons in Your Customer's Brain" explores how the triune brain theory can help marketers better connect with consumers. The book focuses on the reptilian brain, which governs survival instincts and plays a crucial role in decision-making. The authors suggest that marketers can create messages that appeal directly to this part of the brain by using visual, emotionally engaging, and simple messaging. By understanding the three areas of the brain (reptilian, emotional, and rational), marketers can craft strategies that first capture attention and then address more profound needs. Techniques such as storytelling, color psychology, and scarcity are all explored as ways to engage the brain's primal responses. Through this framework, the book shows how businesses can design more effective marketing campaigns by aligning with how consumers' brains process information.

EMBRACE Cultural Needs

BOOK 1: The Theory

Fons Trompenaars and Charles Hampden-Turner's "Riding the Waves of Culture: Understanding Diversity in Global Business" comprehensively explore how cultural differences impact business practices and communication worldwide. The book offers valuable insights into navigating and leveraging cultural diversity for successful global business interactions. The authors present a framework of seven cultural dimensions, such as individualism vs. collectivism or universalism vs. particularism, which help to explain how different cultures approach issues like authority, time, and relationships. The book emphasizes the importance of cultural awareness for managing cross-cultural teams, negotiating, and making decisions in a globalized economy through real-world examples, case studies, and practical applications. Ultimately, "Riding the Waves of Culture" serves as a guide to understanding cultural differences and turning those differences into opportunities, helping business leaders and organizations thrive in international contexts.

Book 2: Marketing Application

E. L. Feit's "The US Multicultural Market: A Marketer's Guide to Understanding and Reaching the New Consumer" is a comprehensive guide to navigating the growing and diverse U.S. consumer market. As the U.S. becomes more multicultural, Feit emphasizes the need for businesses to adapt their marketing strategies to reach Asian-American, African-American, Hispanic-American, and other cultural groups. The book covers demographic shifts, cultural preferences, and how businesses can tailor their messages to resonate with different ethnic audiences. Feit also explores the challenges marketers face, such as overcoming stereotypes and language barriers, while highlighting opportunities for engaging with diverse consumers. The book provides insights into creating effective multicultural marketing campaigns through case studies and practical examples.

Tell a Story of Values

Book 1: The Theory

Simon Sinek's "Start with Why: How Great Leaders Inspire Everyone to Take Action" highlights the importance of starting with "Why"—a clear purpose—to inspire action and loyalty. Sinek's "Golden Circle" framework includes "What" (what a company offers), "How" (how they do it), and "Why" (the core purpose). At the same time, most focus on "What" and "How," Sinek argues that the most successful leaders begin with "Why," connecting values to inspire trust and loyalty. Through examples like Apple and Martin Luther King Jr., he demonstrates how starting with Why aligns actions with purpose, creating emotional connections that drive long-term success.

Book 2: Marketing Application

Seth Godin's "Tribes" argues that leadership gathers people around a shared idea or cause. He suggests that anyone with a passion and a willingness to make an impact can lead a tribe, essentially a community of people united by common interests, values, or goals. The book emphasizes that modern technology, especially the internet, has made it easier to connect with like-minded people and build these tribes, bypassing traditional gatekeepers like media or corporate power structures. Godin encourages readers to embrace the role of leader, focusing on making meaningful connections rather than seeking approval from the masses. He believes tribes are powerful because they create belonging, and leaders can inspire change through these connections. The book shows how brands and individuals can leverage tribal leadership to build loyal followings and drive movements.

Get the Right Code

. . .

BOOK 1: The Theory

Margaret Mark and Carol S. Pearson's "The Hero and the Outlaw" reveals how brands can unlock the unconscious "code" that drives human behavior by aligning with timeless archetypes. These archetypes—like the Hero, the Rebel, or the Lover—tap into universal human desires and emotions, resonating with people on a deeper, often unconscious level. The book shows how storytelling and symbolism rooted in these archetypes can create brands that feel meaningful, inspire loyalty, and stand out in a crowded world. By cracking this unconscious code, brands move beyond selling products—building lasting relationships and identities.

BOOK 2: Marketing Application

Clotaire Rapaille's "The Culture Code" unpacks how cultural values often affect people's thinking, feelings, and actions without their knowledge. It reveals that every culture has a unique "code" driving what people subconsciously desire and how they interpret the world. By understanding these hidden codes, brands can craft messages and experiences that resonate deeply, creating stronger connections and lasting loyalty. The book shows how aligning with cultural codes helps brands stand out, communicate more effectively, and build emotional bonds that lead to lasting success.

MAKE It Easy

BOOK 1: The Theory

Mihaly Csikszentmihalyi's "Flow: The Psychology of

Optimal Experience" introduces the concept of "flow," a state of deep focus and immersion where individuals feel fully engaged and lose track of time. Flow happens when challenges align with one's skill level, creating a balance that avoids boredom or frustration. It brings joy, creativity, and peak performance. The book explains how to cultivate flow through goal-oriented activities, provide immediate feedback, and require focused attention. Csikszentmihalyi also connects flow to overall happiness, arguing that structuring life to maximize these experiences can improve well-being. This timeless work remains a cornerstone for understanding optimal human performance and satisfaction.

Book 2: Marketing Application

Laura Busche's "Brand Psychology: The Art and Science of Building Strong Brands" integrates psychology, design, and marketing to reveal how flow-like experiences make brands memorable and engaging. It delves into creating immersive brand stories, sensory branding, and strategies that align with consumer behavior. Busche highlights techniques to craft strong brand identities across digital and offline channels, emphasizing emotional connections and unique experiences. Using case studies, infographics, and practical exercises, the book provides a toolkit for entrepreneurs and marketers to navigate branding in a digitally connected and highly competitive landscape.

Facilitate Connectivity

Book 1: The Theory

Henry Jenkins' "Transmedia 202: Further Reflections" digs deeper into transmedia storytelling and its impact on how we consume narratives today. He highlights how different media platforms (film, TV, games, etc.) all contribute to a bigger, more immersive story. Each medium stands alone but adds something essential to the whole experience. Jenkins also emphasizes that fans aren't just passive consumers—they actively engage with and help shape the storylines. This level of interaction, he argues, could change the future of media, entertainment, education, and even politics, making narratives more collaborative and expansive. In short, the book goes beyond just entertainment, looking at how convergence impacts how stories unfold across digital platforms, bringing together fans, creators, and industries in a much more dynamic, interactive world.

BOOK 2: Marketing Application

Max Lenderman's "Experience the Message: How Experiential Marketing Is Changing the Brand World" explores how branding moves toward immersive, experience-based marketing. Instead of just pushing products, brands are now focused on creating memorable, emotional connections with customers through experiences like live events, pop-up shops, and interactive campaigns. Lenderman highlights how this shift is about authenticity—brands must engage their customers in real, meaningful ways, inviting them to be part of the brand's story.

This approach isn't just about selling; it's about fostering loyalty by making customers feel personally connected. Using real-world examples, Lenderman shows how experiential marketing can turn a simple transaction into a lasting relationship. The book argues that the future of branding lies in creating experiences that resonate emotionally, helping brands stand out in a crowded market by engaging their audience more deeply and personally.

Emphasize the Authentic

Book 1: The Theory

James H. Gilmore and B. Joseph Pine II's "Authenticity: What Consumers Want" dives into how consumers increasingly value authenticity in their purchasing decisions today. The book explores how businesses can stand out by managing customers' perceptions of authenticity. It emphasizes that it's not just about quality or price but about being "true" to what you claim to be. It identifies five critical genres of authenticity—natural, original, exceptional, referential, and influential—and shows how companies like Starbucks and Disney excel by making authenticity a central part of their brand identity. The authors argue that to meet the rising demand for the "real deal," companies must carefully manage how they present themselves, ensuring that their offerings are genuine and aligned with their stated values. This book provides practical frameworks to help companies craft and implement strategies that resonate with consumers increasingly looking for authentic businesses, from marketing to operations.

Book 2: Marketing Application

Mark Toft, Jay Sunny, and Rich Taylor's "Authenticity: Building a Brand in an Insincere Age" critique how modern marketing often relies on superficial tactics rather than genuine connections. The book argues that many companies fail to align their messaging with their core values, leaving consumers feeling disconnected and skeptical. Toft, Sunny, and Taylor advocate for a more authentic approach, one where brands are clear about their purpose and communicate in a way that resonates emotionally with their audience. The authors emphasize the importance of purpose-driven branding, noting that brands should talk about what they sell and stand for. They urge businesses to avoid "aspirational" advertising that lacks sincerity, instead encouraging them to embrace natural, compelling stories that reflect the values of the brand and its customers. A key takeaway from the book is that authenticity requires conflict—brands should not shy away from addressing tough issues or challenging the status quo. The book presents case studies from companies that have succeeded in being true to their purpose, such as LEGO, Zappos, and HBO. It also shows the pitfalls of inauthenticity, such as the downfall of brands like United Airlines or Facebook. Ultimately, the authors believe authenticity isn't just a buzzword; it's essential for building lasting customer loyalty and standing out in a crowded market.

AFTERWORD

This book isn't meant to have a final word; instead, it's an invitation to keep exploring how brands can become essential. The world of branding is constantly changing—shaped by new technologies, shifting consumer habits, and fresh trends. Throughout the book, we've looked at a mix of classic, well-established brands, and newer, rising stars. These examples show us how different brands have stayed relevant by adapting to analog and digital markets. Whether it's big names that have been around for decades or up-and-coming disruptors, they all share the ability to evolve and find ways to remain unique in an ever-crowded space.

We've seen how these brands leverage creativity, storytelling, and innovative strategies to stay connected with their audiences and how they've adapted to both traditional and digital markets. The key takeaway is that branding is not a one-time thing; it's an ongoing process. The rules constantly shift, and what works today might not work tomorrow. That's why this book is meant to be a guide you can keep returning to. The included bibliography opens the door to more resources, giving you more ways to dive deeper into the strategies and ideas discussed here.

As the line between analog and digital continues to blur, brands must stay flexible and forward-thinking. The digital world changes fast, but the analog world still holds power. Today's most successful brands know how to move between these two worlds, mixing the best of both to engage with their customers in fresh ways. The examples here show just how this balance plays out in real time.

Ultimately, branding is about an ongoing conversation, not a fixed solution. The journey to becoming a unique and essential brand doesn't have a finish line—it's something that brands should work on continuously. This book serves as a starting point, but the future of branding is still ahead of us and will keep evolving.

ACKNOWLEDGMENTS

My gratitude and love go to my wife, Monica, for his serene presence, wisdom, and manuscript feedback.

My unconditional love and appreciation are to my children, their spouses, and grandchildren.

I want to express my gratitude to all my colleagues who have supported my ideas and shared their wisdom along my professional journey.

In closing, I hope this book becomes an essential companion in your marketing journey.

www.ingramcontent.com/pod-product-compliance
Lightning Source LLC
Chambersburg PA
CBHW071024240526
45469CB00006BD/2085